THE HAPPINESS EDGE

THE EIGHT PRINCIPLES OF HAPPINESS TO GAIN COMPETITIVE ADVANTAGE IN BUSINESS AND LIFE

VISHAL PANDEY

TABLE OF CONTENTS

PART I

INTRODUCTION

I was 18 years old when I had that "something is wrong" moment. My close friend was arrested by the police. A lot of chaos was going around me. There was a lot of confusion.

I had no money and was living on my own. I always thought that if I could improve my financial situation, and my friend would come back to me, everything would be great right now. Life would be perfect.

Eventually, he *did* come back and I *did* make money. At 18 years old, my concept of happiness was simple - just have enough money for food, clothes, CDs, and arcade games. Glory days of youth. Wasn't it nice?

I was so happy. I got the money and was playing Tekken 3 at the arcade mall. Awesome game! My favorite characters were King and Eddie. I was having the time of my life playing that game. But at the same time, I was still feeling kind of depressed.

I thought "whatever... let's do something else." I went to buy new clothes. Then I got some music CDs. I love to eat at restaurants. When I was young, eating out was like a treat that I got from my parents. I loved it. Now I don't eat out often but back then I loved going to the food court. So I go to the food court and order a pizza. After I finished the pizza, I ordered a burger and ate that.

But the funny thing was - I was *still* not feeling good.

I thought "let's get some noodles." I ordered noodles and ate them. Then I thought let's eat something sweet. I got ice cream and I ate and I ate and I ate till the point I was ready to vomit.

I was sitting at the table in this food count, so full that I was ready to vomit. I lay there, my head resting on the table, and these words came up in my mind, "Something is wrong."

"Something is wrong."

I had everything that I was looking for. At the age of 18, I had all the success that I wanted. I was sitting there and thinking, "Something is wrong".

There are two ways to be really unhappy. One is when you don't get what you want. And the other way to be really unhappy is by *getting what you want.*

I was unfortunate enough to get what I wanted.

Can you imagine what celebrities go through in their lives? They have all the fame, all the love, all the money they could ever want... and go completely crazy.

Think of the insanity that they must feel. Because at least when your conditions are not right, you can blame your conditions for your unhappiness. But when you are unhappy, even in ideal conditions, there is no one to blame but yourself. It can make you insane.

As time passed, I had to go through many good and bad situations. I did everything I could to change my situations into positive. I had a good income. I was living in a great place. My business was doing great. Everything was good. Finally, I am sitting at this beautiful beach, sipping soda in a nice, perfect afternoon and everybody around me is looking so happy... and I am thinking "Something is wrong. I am unhappy. Why am I unhappy?"

"I have made it. I got what I wanted. Why am I still unhappy? Something is very wrong."

These thoughts stayed with me for a while and honestly speaking, it can drive you crazy.

People around you are unhappy because they don't really have what they want, and that's ok. But if you have what you want and still you are not happy, something is wrong.

Let's say you get all the money that you want and all the success that you want, that would make you pretty happy, right?

Everyone had that thought at some point.

Angus Deaton and Daniel Kahneman of Princeton University conducted a research on the relationship between money and happiness.

After an analysis of more than 450,000 responses to the Gallup-Healthways Well-Being Index, researchers found that the increase in income results in increased life satisfaction and emotional well-being, but to a certain limit. There is no increase in life satisfaction, happiness and emotional well-being beyond an annual income of ~ $75,000.

In other words, after you achieve an annual income of ~75,000 USD, a further increase in income would not directly result in more happiness and satisfaction.

I was at that point. I got the money. I got the success. And I was still unhappy.

I was very stressed out. I was having trouble sleeping. I didn't feel like this earlier when the times were tough and I was grinding for success. The real stress came after I got all the success I wanted.

It was at that point I decided to understand happiness. It became an obsession for me. After reading hundreds of books and studies on happiness conducted all over the world, some of the key points came up again and again.

Several studies in the *Psychological Bulletin* found that happiness doesn't follow success. In fact, it's the other way around. Happiness *leads* to success.

Happiness comes first.

According to research, happiness increases the performance of people and drives them to seek and achieve new goals.

Sonja Lyubomirsky, Ph.D. suggests, "When people feel happy, they tend to feel confident, optimistic, and energetic and others find them likable and sociable."

Happy people also feel negative emotions and face difficulties in their path, but they respond differently to tough situations than the average person.

While factors like intelligence, education, fitness, skills, and peer support also play a role in determining the success of an individual, happy people are more likely to have higher income, fulfilling relationships, superior work ethic, compassion towards others and a healthier lifestyle."

In this book, we are going to completely debunk the myth that success creates happiness and why it's the other way around. You will also learn eight groundbreaking principles to leverage the power of happiness in your work and personal life.

HAPPINESS IS AN ASSET

For thousands of years, people thought that the earth is flat. It looks flat, it feels flat, and so it must be flat. It was discovered later that the earth is actually spherical. It shocked everyone at the time and fundamentally changed our understanding of the earth.

Currently, a comparable shift in the concept of happiness is in progress. For generations, we are led to believe that success and achievements are the creators of happiness. When we become successful, we will be happy. The more achievement we have, the happier we would become.

Now, with the new developments in psychology, a new truth is surfacing – happiness leads to success. Not the other way around. Happy people are more ambitious, motivated, persistent and active than average individuals.

Sadly, despite hundreds of studies advocating the powerful effect of positivity, our society is still pushing the agenda of "no pain, no gain" mentality to the average individual. Business corporations are actively promoting hustle and grind culture to their employees.

While there is certainly a place for work ethic, the aspect of happiness cannot be ignored. Studies after studies have shown the measurable improvements in the performance of individuals and businesses, after adopting the culture of "working happily".

The most successful people in the world know the importance of happiness and how it gives them an "edge" in their professional and personal life. You are about to get a deeper understanding of the relationship between happiness & success, and how to use it to your advantage.

Happiness and success

We are led to believe that success comes first. Once you become successful, you can be happy. There is no other way.

If that was true, then everyone would just work non-stop until they achieve their goal and live happily ever after. We all know, and several pieces of research prove, that it doesn't work that way. If we look around, we will find several examples of people who had all the money, all the fame, all the admiration they wanted, and still resort to drugs and alcohol to feel happy.

A study examined the effect of happiness on some participants' career. 19 Years after entering college, participants were measured on three criteria – current income, job satisfaction, and unemployment history.

Its analysis shows that individuals with a higher happiness rating at college entry have a higher current income and a higher job satisfaction rating and are less likely to have been unemployed than individuals with a lower happiness rating.

(Study Link - https://link.springer.com/article/10.1023/A:1019672513984)

It is not just higher income, Gallup-Healthways Well-Being Index shows that unhappy employees take 15 more sick-leaves in a year. Happy people have better health, better immune system and are resistant to mental disorders like depression & anxiety.

Happier people are also found to be more productive than average. In a 2010 study, James K. Harter and colleagues concluded that low job-satisfaction and happiness at the workplace resulted in poorer bottom-line performance. When people don't care about their jobs or their employers, they don't show up consistently, they are less productive, or their work quality suffers.

In an independent research done by Teresa Amabile and Steven Kramer, around 12,000 electronic diary entries from 238 working professionals in seven different companies were collected. The analysis of these entries revealed the inner work lives of employees. The results were shocking. In one-third of the 12,000 diary entries, the employees were unhappy, unmotivated or both.

Research shows that the emotional life of employees has a big impact on their creativity, productivity, commitment, and problem-solving ability. Employees are more likely to have new ideas and insights when they feel happier.

Conventional wisdom suggests that pressure improves performance, but actual data shows that workers perform better when they are *happily* engaged in what they do.

The role of stress

Our brain behaves differently under the influence of negative emotions like stress. Suppose you are trekking through a forest and a vicious bear starts charging at you, it will immediately trigger "fight or flight" response in your body. The brain will shut down any physical processes unnecessary in this situation and direct all energy, oxygen and blood flow to legs and other organs which will allow you to run away to safety.

This is a biological mechanism built inside every human being. This is why you cannot think properly when you are under a lot of stress at work or home. The more intense the emotion, the more distorted your mind would become.

There is a lot of truth in the old saying "Never make a decision when you are angry." Intense emotions like anger, fear, and anxiety significantly compromise your ability to process information and make rational decisions. It would be wise to time-out and get relaxed before tackling any critical issue at work or home.

Criticism at work

One of the primary causes of stress & unsatisfaction at work is receiving criticism. To have a relaxed and happy mindset at the workplace, we need to know how to effectively deal with all the criticism - justified or unjustified - coming your way.

Criticism is difficult to face because many people associate the work performance of an individual to their worth as a person. This is absolutely ridiculous and yet it's the reason for so much conflict in the workplace.

This section aims to provide you with guidelines on how to deal with criticism and avoid conflict while maintaining your self-respect and peace of mind.

Rights in criticism

First of all, you should know the rights you and the other person have when it comes to criticism.

1. Other people - especially your teammates and your seniors - have the right to criticize your performance. If you do not accept this truth, you will always view their criticism as a personal attack on yourself.

2. You have the right to be criticized for your work performance BUT not in a manner which lowers your worth as a person. There should only be criticism for your work performance. Nothing else. No put-downs, or made to look small, or endure personal attacks, or receiving criticism in front of other co-workers.

With that said, let's look at exactly what to do when receiving criticism.

How to deal with criticism?

1. If the criticism is valid:

If you made a genuine mistake and the criticism is justified, then just listen to the other person and try to understand their situation. Keep your composure and assure the other person that you will not repeat it in the future. Keep things light and simple. Focus more on listening and understanding the other person. Calmly return to your work.

2. If the criticism is unjustified:

If you do not agree with the criticism, then speak your mind. Explain to them why you think differently. Say things like, "the way I see it, this report is not needed today." or "In my opinion, this report should have been prepared by tomorrow."

Using words like "The way I see it..." or "In my opinion ..." or "In my estimation ..." clarifies your thought process to the other person and builds up mutual understanding between the both of you.

Just make sure to remain calm and composed rather than aggressive.

3. If it is a personal attack:

If the criticism from someone is more focused on you than the actual work, call them out on it. Bring to their attention that this is not acceptable. Do not be aggressive, but remain firm.

"I agree with your criticism about the project delay but please do not make it a personal attack."

"I agree that my sales numbers are not up to the mark, but I would prefer it if you don't make it personal."

Calling out a personal attack is very effective in defusing the situation quickly. Once you put the light on it, people tend to back off. If they keep on pushing, they risk coming across as jerks.

4. When you are unsure about the criticism

If you are not sure what the criticism is about, then ask the other person to elaborate. Ask them to give you an example.

Just make sure to ask in a normal, calm tone of voice. Say "I would find it helpful if you can give me an example of what you mean."

Do not be aggressive or challenging. Don't say, "You are not making any sense. Either explain what you mean or stop wasting my time."

If you keep your composure, you will influence the other person to respond calmly as well.

Resolve the conflict

Take the initiative to end the conversation in harmony. Try to resolve the conflict by discussing different options and come up with a mutual agreement that's win-win for both sides involved.

While many organizations use the performance feedback system to improve the productivity of their employees, it may come across as criticism. The guidelines provided above will allow you to deal with criticism with confidence while maintaining your happiness & composure.

The power of positivity

Recent research shows that happiness gives us a real edge on the competition. Positive emotions like happiness and gratitude flood the brain with a plethora of hormones which play a part in sharpening cognitive functions in the brain:

* **Endorphins** reduce stress and help you relax. As a direct result, they help fight anxiety and depression. They also reduce pain & discomfort, enhance pleasure & improve self-esteem.

* **Serotonin** regulates your hunger, makes you sleep better, and influence your mood. All of these go hand-in-hand to make us feel happier, relaxed, and positive.

* **Dopamine** signals reward and pleasure centers in our brain. It controls our motivation levels and thus, determines how much action we take towards our goals.

These Neuro-chemicals not only make us feel good but activate the learning centers of our brains. We process information better, connect the dots faster, and gain new ideas & insights.

The advancements in psychology and brain research are repeatedly showing the significance of happiness in the overall quality of life for an individual, and our society is slowly beginning to embrace this idea.

Twitter offers its employees free meals, yoga classes and even unlimited vacations for some. SquareSpace offers various benefits, like comprehensive health insurance, vacation perks, recreational clubs, fully-stocked kitchens, equity options, and game rooms.

Google provides free meals and cooking classes, on-site gyms, gorgeous office space, massage therapy, employee trips, financial bonuses, and a pet-friendly environment.

However, there is still a lot of work to be done before "happiness as a competitive edge" is fully accepted by our community.

A change is needed and it requires a substantial effort to make it widespread.

A powerful exercise to increase your happiness and positivity

The last section of this book provides 51 different ways to increase happiness in your day. However, I would like to mention one specific exercise that made a big impact on the amount of happiness I experience on a daily basis. Best of all, it takes less than five minutes.

When you wake up in the morning, write down five things you are grateful for.

For example, when you sit down in the morning to drink at the office, take out a notebook and write five things you are grateful for in your life. Do it daily for 21 days.

A few pointers for this exercise:

1. These five things could either be big or small, it doesn't matter. It could even be something as simple as "I am grateful for this morning coffee. Thank you."

No matter how small or simple the thing you are grateful for, it still counts. As you continue to do this exercise, your creativity would kick in and you'll come up with various things to feel grateful for.

2. It is important to write down these five things in a piece of paper (notebook, diary, notepad, etc.). Writing them digitally in electronic devices do not count. They should be written on a physical paper with a pen.

This is an important step. Writing on a paper with pen influences our brain very differently than typing on a keyboard.

According to research done by Anne Mangen at the University of Stavanger, writing by hand strengthens the learning process. When typing on a keyboard or touch screen, this process may be impaired.

"Writing by hand (pen and paper) strengthens the learning process. When we type on a keyboard or touch screen, this process may be impaired. Neurophysiologists have conducted a research which confirms the significance of these differences.

While handwriting, our brain receives feedback from our motor actions, together with the sensation of touching a pen and paper. This kind of feedback is very different from the one we receive when touching and typing on a keyboard."

Make sure you use a pen and paper while doing this exercise.

Tip: Keep a pen & notebook at the place where you drink morning coffee (or at any other place you selected for this exercise). It would be very convenient to just pick up the pen & paper and start writing.

3. If you are not in the mood to do this exercise, tell yourself that it takes less than five minutes. It would be over before you finish your coffee.

4. You have to do this daily for 21 days. It takes 3 weeks for our brain to develop new neurological pathways. In other words, it takes 3 weeks for the brain to rewire itself and create the habit of positivity and happiness.

Do the exercise every day for three weeks.

Additional step: Go deeper

Write a few sentences about any of the five things you wrote down. You can go more in-depth. Explain *why* you are grateful for it. What do you appreciate the most about it? How it affected you positively? How thankful you are for it?

This will deepen your sense of gratitude. You will feel even more grateful for those things. We don't appreciate the things we already have in our life. We get caught up in our fast-paced life and forget how blessed we truly are.

This step will draw out the exact reasons *why* you are grateful for something and deepen the sense of thankfulness in your mind.

This step is optional but it speeds up the change process and feels really good. Try it yourself.

This 5-gratitude exercise made a significant impact on the amount of happiness & positivity I experienced in my daily life. I shared it with several people and they all love it! It is a great way to train our brain to focus on the positives of life, which is an absolute necessity today.

"Gratitude is the healthiest of all human emotions. The more you express gratitude for what you have, the more likely you will have even more to express gratitude for." - Zig Ziglar

THE CORE ELEMENT

If you are overstressed with a heavy workload, then this chapter is for you.

Multitasking causes stress, confusion, and a drop in creativity

In our society, multitasking is viewed as a good thing. It is considered as a sign that a person is super busy and productive.

But being busy and being productive are two different things.

In reality, multitasking creates a lot of stress, reduces your creativity and compromises the quality of your work. When carrying out any important assignment, multitasking may be your worst enemy.

Let's look at a few key reasons why you should try to avoid multitasking.

1. Multitasking causes stress

Studies show that multitasking is stressful. It may cause a lot of strain on your mind & body. When your mind is working fulltime on several things at once, you become stressed.

And when you focus on one single objective with no distractions, it's a relief. You'll feel more in control and on top of things, instead of feeling overburdened and overwhelmed.

2. Multitasking compromises creativity

Creative thoughts and ideas tend to vanish as quickly as they pop up. They have a very short lifespan. When you are busy with several things at once, other thoughts will dominate the creative thought you had. It will slip away and be gone forever.

3. Multitasking wastes time

We think of multitasking as a way to save time, but it does the opposite. It often wastes time. When your attention is divided, you fumble and make mistakes, or the quality of work is not up to the mark. Several times you have to go back and re-do the work.

4. Multitasking reduces the quality

When we do several things at once, the quality of work gets compromised significantly. While multitasking, your mind will be too distracted to come up with creative ideas to solve a problem or finish a task. Switching back and forth will also make you lose your train of thought, resulting in cutting corners and thus lowering the overall quality of your work.

5. Multitasking reduces productivity

Multitasking entails handling several tasks at once and switching between them quickly. It prevents you from focusing on any task for too long. According to a study conducted by David Mayer Ph.D. in 2001, multitasking can reduce your productivity by up to 40 percent!

The search for happiness in work-life

Modern technology has completely changed our world. It opened several doors and provided endless opportunities, gave rise to new and improved ways to finish tasks and make our lives easier.

As thrilling technological advances may be, they also came with some downsides. There are *wayyy* more information and choices in front of us at any given moment. It's overwhelming. The more technology we adopt to simplify our work (and life), the more complicated it gets. The more we try, the more we get tangled in the technological web.

The biggest example is the internet. It was created with the intent to share meaningful information and to facilitate education. Along with providing endless opportunities, it gave birth to some of the most addictive distractions we have ever seen - social media, online video games, adult sites, etc.

We have so much to do... in so little time, and yet we are surrounded by distractions. It creates a lot of stress, confusion, and mental chaos. We want to live a happy, peaceful life. For that, we have to keep our work-life under control. We must adopt a different way to get our work done that is smooth, calm and stress-free.

A solution is needed

What is the best way to handle tasks in our work life?

The answer is: Only focus on your **core element** at any given moment.

Your "core element" is the ONE task which is the most important AND most urgent at this moment.

It has to be both - important and urgent. It has to be done, and done quickly.

If a task is important but not urgent, schedule it for later. If a task is urgent but not important, delegate it to someone else. Right now, you should only focus on a task which is important AND urgent, i.e. your core element.

Focus on it with your complete attention until it gets done. Do not focus on anything else.

All successful people know the importance of focusing on a single task for a period of time. According to Napoleon Hill, author of *Think and Grow Rich*, intensely focusing on a single objective is the starting point for achieving all success, money, and happiness you desire.

This idea has changed the lives of millions of people and will continue to transform even more lives in the future. It's time you embrace this idea as well.

Benefits of focusing on the core element

1. Lowers stress at work

Focusing on the core element helps in dealing with the biggest problem we face at work: stress. We experience stress when we take on more than we can handle.

Focusing on one task at a time frees up your brain's processing power and gets the work done on time. It significantly reduces stress levels and the feeling of being overwhelmed.

Also, finishing the work efficiently means you get more time for hobbies, family or anything else you may like, which is a nice bonus.

2. Cut through the clutter

Decluttering is the art of reducing something to its simplest form... so that you cannot take anything away anymore. Focusing on the core element takes away everything that is not essential. It makes your work (and your life) a lot simpler. You feel a lot more calm & peaceful when you ignore distractions and don't make work more complicated than it has to be.

3. It improves clarity

When you are focused on the core element, you will think long & hard before committing to a new task or project. You'll evaluate every new activity for whether it is helping you in moving towards your main objective or not.

It forces you to become very clear about your chief objective. You will have to know _exactly_ what your end goal is and how you will go about it. You will stay on track and build momentum towards your goals.

4. Revives your mental energy

When you focus on the core element, you don't try to take on multiple things at once. You only have a single objective. You don't have to solve every problem. You just need to solve one.

You have fewer things to think about, which frees up your mental energy. You will have enough mental juice to tackle difficult challenges that may come across your way.

You'll achieve more in less time while feeling alive, energetic, positive, and raring to go.

How to implement the principle of the core element in your work life?

Now we get to the core of this chapter - how to design your work life around your core element and let nothing distract you.

1. Align your lifestyle with your core element

Once you have selected your core element (your primary objective), you must change your lifestyle so it allows you to work hard on your goal. Taking focused action requires a lot of energy, concentration, time, effort, and discipline. It's not easy.

(It's called HARD WORK after all)

To do it successfully over long periods of time, you'll need to change your lifestyle into something which supports you. The way we normally spend our daily life, determines our energy level, discipline, mood, and willpower significantly.

For example, if you eat food containing lots of sugar at breakfast, you will have an energy crash mid-morning and struggle with energy for the rest of the day.

Sugar gives an instant burst of energy, but soon your energy drops to an even lower level than before. (You can Google the effects of sugar on your energy and mood.)

Similarly, frequent late nights, drinking lots of alcohol, eating processed foods— all take a toll on your mind and body, making you less energetic and dulling your concentration.

You must take control of your lifestyle, so that you feel alive, energetic, positive, and raring to go!

A good lifestyle means the following:

• Good nutrition

• Quantity (& quality) of sleep

• Physical exercise

• Your peers. Surround yourself with positive, upbeat people.

• Read books and success stories

• Cut down negative influences like TV, magazines, toxic people, etc.

Get your lifestyle in order. When you do this, you will feel great most of the time. You will have a balanced mental and physical condition to focus on your core element.

2. Plan your mood and energy levels in advance

Some people have more energy in the morning, while others do their best work at night. Whatever your preferred time to work is, you need to schedule your day so that the majority of your most important work falls on the time of the day when you perform your best.

For example, I am a morning person. I tend to do my best in the morning. I can also work in the afternoon and night, but the quality & quantity of my morning work is far superior.

The same thing goes for your energy levels. Our energy levels tend to fluctuate during the day. Some people feel more energetic in the morning and others during the day or late at night... Plan your day around it.

Try working at different times of the day to find your preferred time in which you feel most energetic, and schedule your work at that time.

This simple step will increase the quality of your focus tremendously. As stated earlier, when you take care of your health, mood, influences, etc., you will feel energetic most of the time during the day. In other words, your "peak performance time" window will get bigger.

When you plan your activity in "peak performance" time (which has increased); you will be able to maintain your focus for a much longer duration.

3. What to do when you feel overwhelmed?

It's easy to get overwhelmed by seeing how much work you have to do. You start doubting whether you can ever finish the work required to achieve the goal.

This line of thought reduces our motivation, and we subconsciously began to delay the actions we need to take. This was a HUGE problem I faced every time I went after a big goal. I found it's not only me, but everyone is facing the same problem.

After much trial and error, I found an effective solution to this problem.

Focus on doing your current task (which is your core element) as best as you can, and have faith that you did the best possible thing you could do for obtaining your goal in the future.

That's it! Just fully concentrate on your current action and do it in the best way possible. Don't think about the future now, as it will distract you from your current task. Doing your best work now is the biggest step you can take towards your goal.

Leave the rest to faith. You did your part in the best way possible.

Now, sometimes you will feel overwhelmed again when you think about how much more you have to do. You will begin to question yourself—"Is worth it?", "Am I doing it right?", "Will it work?", "Is my work good enough?"

It will be very scary and disheartening. But realize that taking action on your core element with 100% effectiveness is the best possible thing you can do, and it's the ONLY variable you can control. No one else could have done anything more. Even the most successful and richest people struggle with this from time to time.

That's the most anyone can do. So, be proud of yourself. You took the biggest possible step towards your goal.

4. Plan your week, month and year

The next step is to plan your activity and focus for the entire next week, month and possibly year. Decide the number of hours you will spend working on your core element, and fit time for it in your day.

Reminder: Try to plan your work at the time when you feel most energetic and focused.

People, who don't fit time for this activity, keep on delaying the work hour after hour and end up doing little to no work done. Do the opposite. Schedule time in which you will take action daily. This will help you avoid procrastination. You will not delay work because it is scheduled. Either you do it or you don't.

There is no chance of "I will do it later syndrome," which is one of the most common obstacles people face when doing work.

Conclusion: Schedule time for your core element. It makes a big difference in the long term.

5. Follow through even if you are not in the mood

After you schedule time for the core element, follow through no matter what. Always do your best. It takes discipline from you. No matter how you are feeling, no matter what excuse your mind is giving you—"Just leave it," "I am not in the mood," "I just want to see this episode on TV," "My friends are going out. I want to go too."

Ignore everything and just start doing your work. If you are REALLY not in the mood to do your work, you will have a 'bad' start. But instead of stopping, keep working. Initially, your mind will resist, but don't stop.

After a little while, your mind will stop resisting the work and accept the fact that work HAS to be done. Then you will be able to work with full focus and effectiveness.

6. Cultivating willpower and discipline

Sometimes 'pushing yourself' is not enough. Maybe you just can't push yourself that much. In that case, you need more willpower to push yourself through excuses & bad emotions and do the work.

Some people say discipline is more important. I beg to differ. I believe if you have enough willpower you will be able to maintain a disciplined life easily. Think of willpower as fuel for discipline. You won't be able to maintain discipline if your willpower is lacking.

In her excellent book *Maximum Willpower*, Kelly McGonigal says willpower is like a muscle. It gets exhausted with use. The more discipline or willpower requiring activities we do, our willpower reserves keeps on reducing.

If it reaches a very low level, then it will be very difficult to fight with excuse-making and procrastination. Thankfully, there are ways to recharge and even strengthen your willpower reserve. The easiest and the most effective way to increase your willpower is to meditate for 10-15 minutes daily.

I believe this simple breathing exercise is a MUST for everyone who aspires for success. Do meditation daily and within a month, you will start noticing increased willpower and countless other benefits like - increased calmness, emotional balance, concentration, focus, happiness, and reduced stress & negative thoughts.

Once you start seeing its benefits, you would be surprised why someone didn't tell you about it earlier.

Now before we start, let me tell you that the core practice of meditation had no attachment with any religion. At it very core, the meditation is about focusing on your breath for a short period of time. We are not concerned with spirituality here.

While meditation can be a powerful spiritual practice, you always have an option of not attaching it with any religion and still get the practical, daily life benefits of increased willpower and discipline.

It's very easy to do and take only 10 to 15 minutes a day to get the full benefits.

Effortless meditation exercise

a) Set an alarm for 10 minutes.

b) Sit comfortably on a chair, keeping your back relaxed & somewhat upright. Use a cushion if you need to. We are not looking for a perfectly upright back posture.

c) Close your eyes and start noticing your breath coming in and out. Notice it effortlessly: when it enters in your nostrils to when it goes in your belly, the movement of your stomach going up and down, etc. Do not try hard. Just notice your breath coming in & going out. Be relaxed.

d) Eventually, your mind will start thinking about something. You will get lost in your thoughts. You lose focus on your breath and start dwelling on the thought itself. It's Ok.

e) Whenever you catch yourself focusing on your thoughts instead of being aware of your breath, gently and calmly shift your focus to your breath.

f) Soon you will lose your focus again and get lost in thoughts. Relax & simply shift your focus to your breath calmly.

g) Keep doing this for 10 minutes till your alarm rings.

Note: Don't force yourself to keep your mind empty all the time. The mind will think and that's what we want. Actually, willpower gets stronger when you keep shifting your focus from your thoughts to your breath. This to-and-fro of awareness is what strengthens willpower muscles. It's like a gym for your mind.

This simple breathing exercise will increase your willpower levels to astronomical levels. Its effectiveness is unmatched. I would even confess that I would not be able to finish this book if it wasn't for meditation. In our society, our daily life has become so demanding that we end up having a very low reserve of willpower.

This simple exercise is the answer. It will replenish the lost supply of willpower and even increase its capacity. Highly, highly recommended.

It is up to you now.

The stress at work has a huge impact on our happiness and positivity. You have just gotten a potent piece of information to keep your work-related stress under control. When you apply the principle of the core element, you will experience more peace, joy, creativity, and fulfillment in your work. You'll start becoming a more positive, happier version of yourself.

Isn't that something we all want?

"It's not the load that breaks you down, it's the way you carry it." - Lou Holtz

FORWARD MOMENTUM

Einstein said that insanity is *'doing the same thing over and over and expecting a different result'*. I believe it also entails a secret to achieving great success.

"Success is doing the right thing over and over and expecting a good result."

When we see people achieving great success, it is tempting to believe their success was overnight. We try to find the one thing they did to achieve success and happiness. But we cannot find it.

"They must have kept it a secret."

"I think it's their luck."

"They had connections."

"They know something *that* we don't."

"They must have been accepted by the Illuminati."

It's crazy what we come up with when we can't find why somebody is successful. We try to find the missing link but to no avail.

What is the secret?

Are they more intelligent? Do they have more information?

Have you ever learned to ski, drive a car, cook your favorite meal, or play guitar? Then you know that knowledge, on its own, is simply not enough.

Have you ever seen two people who are similar to each other but one achieves more success than the other? They might have similar education, age, fitness, ambition, etc. But one outperforms the other by a large margin.

Why is that?

Success is not about being more intelligent or luckier or ambitious. There is one quality above everything else. And that is *consistency*.

There's a famous quote, "The world rewards action, not thoughts." And yet so many people are stuck with overanalyzing the situation. They want to figure out each and every little nuance and piece of information before starting something new. They overwhelmed themselves by the information available and never take any action. This is called "paralysis by analysis". They never come out of the collecting information, planning and organizing stage.

No amount of theory can prepare you for what's to come. Only by taking action, you get feedback about what's right and what's wrong. What works for you and what doesn't?

One of my friends, Anita wanted to learn driving. Being an engineer, she has a tendency to analyze everything before she does something. She only takes action when she is convinced that she has enough information.

Before taking the driving classes, she would sit in my car and ask me several questions about how to drive, "Ok so this is the accelerator, it moves the car forward." , "What's the use of the clutch?" , "So this stick is how you shift gears?"

Being a helpful friend, I used to hide my annoyance and answer all her questions. The funny thing is, she was reluctant to join driving classes. She said, "First, I want to know how everything works in a car. I will not make mistakes if I am well prepared beforehand."

She drove me crazy for about two weeks by her non-stop questions. Finally, I convinced her that she knows everything now and join a class.

I was so interested in how she will do in the first driving class that I went with her. Deep inside I knew that everyone finds it hard on the first day, but she is really bright and actually knows what does what in a car.

So I was genuinely interested to see how she does.

The instructor told her the basics of driving and she just listened. She knew where the clutch was, press left & up to shift to the first gear, where the accelerator is located, etc.

I had told her everything in the past two weeks. She knew everything about driving a car.

After the instructor told her to start the car, she pressed the auto-start button to start the car. Then she pressed the clutch pedal and shifted to the first gear. She slowly released the clutch and pressed the accelerator.

The car VIOLENTLY jumped forward and WHACK!

Engine shuts down!

No amount of information and weeks of theory could prepare her for the HARDEST aspect of learning to drive - how to time the release of the clutch while pushing down the accelerator AND keeping both eyes on the road AND handling the steering all at the same time.

It was crazy!

She knew the location of everything and how it worked. She knew all the theory.

But she never actually did it earlier.

Taking action in the real world is a lot different than the information world we immerse ourselves in. Anita, despite knowing how things worked in a car, was struggling to start the car. And even when she managed to start the car, it was shutting down when she slowed down, or when she shifted gears.

The clutch-accelerator timing takes PRACTICE. Shifting gears while keeping both eyes on the road takes PRACTICE. Reversing the car into parallel parking takes PRACTICE.

No amount of information or theory can replace action. When we take action, we find what works for us and what doesn't, what we need to change, and what we need to learn.

"One hour of action will teach you more than a week of learning theory." - **An old proverb**

As for Anita, driving the car for 3 days taught her more than two weeks of gathering information about it.

Fast forward a couple of months... she became an excellent driver.

We are not rewarded for what we know. We are rewarded for what we do.

What about procrastination?

There is a tendency in many people (including me) to delay the task which needs to be done. There is a name for it - procrastination. It's a buzz word today. We share our crazy procrastination stories with our friends. We all laugh at it. But we also want to know how to get rid of it.

Most of the time, procrastination or the inability to take action stems from *fear of failure*. Ask a guy, wanting to approach women in a bar, why he could not approach anyone. He will say, "Because I will get rejected." In other words, "I will fail."

Ask a student who is procrastinating on writing a report. She will reply, "I don't want to write it." If you dig deeper and ask her why, she will reply, "I am not good at it." She is afraid of failing to do a good job.

When a person accepts the possibility of both success and failure, they release all mental roadblocks to taking action. Being afraid to fail when taking action is like driving a car with the handbrakes on. It results in a lot of wasted energy.

People who are action takers are not afraid to fail. Why? Because every failure tells them, "Something is not working. Change it." They learn from their mistakes. They learn from the criticism. They learn from the failure.

It makes them improve their craft, develop new skills, and change their approach. They use failure as a stepping stone to success.

Don't try to forget the mistakes you made in the past, but don't dwell on them also. Close the door on your past failures. Do not let them have any of your energy, or any of your time, or any of your space.

Once you have learned a lesson from a past mistake, let it go. It served its purpose. You don't need it anymore.

How action is related to happiness?

With the rise of "mindfulness" culture, experts will tell you that happiness comes from "being", not doing. While there is certainly a place for presence and meditation in our lives, the significant impact of taking action cannot be understated.

The reason is simple: Taking action makes progress. Progress results in happiness.

 Contrary to the popular belief, happiness doesn't come after you achieve your goal. Happiness is in the journey itself. Happiness is becoming the person capable of tackling various challenges that come up. Happiness is making progress towards something you desire.

After you achieve your intended desire, you look for something else to move towards. You set new goals.

For example, you work hard and gather enough money to buy your dream car. You feel ecstatic! You feel amazing! But after a month or so, your new car suddenly doesn't excite you anymore. A new idea comes in your mind, "Hey, what if I get a promotion? How would feel?"

This happens subconsciously. We quickly jump from one goal to another. Not because we are greedy. But because deep inside, we know that *making progress* is what makes us happy, not the end goal.

In fact, achieving the result is often anti-climactic. You think, "That's it??! I worked so hard for THIS???" Deep inside you recognize the fact that *you were happier while you were progressing towards your goal*.

It is one of the universal laws of human nature that our society tries so hard to suppress. Since childhood, we are taught that happiness comes *after* success. First, you achieve your goals, and then you become happy.

In practice, it is exactly the opposite. You feel happier *while* you are taking action. You feel happier when you are *making progress*. Happiness and taking action are so intertwined with each other that we cannot separate one from the other.

Action makes progress. Progress creates happiness. And as we discussed in chapter one - *Happiness is an asset* - happiness boosts our motivation to take even more action and achieve even more success. It is an upward, self-sustaining cycle of happiness, action, and success.

So, if action and making progress have such a significant effect on our happiness then how can we make the process of taking action a bit easier and adopt a progressive lifestyle?

Forward Momentum

Let me introduce you to the third principle - *forward momentum*.

Forward momentum is the "flow" you have when you are taking action consistently. It's like if you are already going to the gym 5 days a week, it will not be difficult to workout 6 days a week. Because you are already taking action, you have forward momentum.

That is why starting a new project is so hard. It takes a lot more effort to initiate something. But once it picks up the momentum, it becomes easier to maintain.

It's much easier to keep a ball rolling, then to get it moving from a standstill.

This is very useful for achieving success, happiness, and fulfillment. Let's see how.

Forward momentum and happiness

The age-old belief that happiness comes from getting more stuff - a bigger house, a faster car, a larger bank account, etc. - is a myth.

It is simply not correct.

When you achieve something, you feel pleasure. It makes you feel good for a while. But those good feelings do not last. Remember when you brought a new car or a new dress, how happy you felt? You were ecstatic. But after a short period of time, the excitement slowly faded away. Your shiny car or that fabulous dress stopped making you feel excited.

This is true for everything you may achieve in life. Even earning millions of dollars, winning the admiration of millions of people, marrying an attractive spouse, and getting six-pack abs gets old quickly. They will not give you lasting happiness that you are looking for.

Actually, happiness is never about *what* you achieve. Real happiness is about the person you become who *can* achieve their goals. Happiness comes from taking on challenges and coming out victorious, facing obstacles and overcoming them, confronting problems and solving them.

Happiness comes from *being* a progressive person - a person who goes for what they want and make efforts to achieve it.

Lasting happiness and fulfillment never come *after* achieving the outcome. It comes from the *journey* to that outcome. Your journey is the reward itself.

Let me share a true story. My friend Naveen wanted to get into the real estate sales business because of its lucrative income. He said, "Vishal, I want to get rich."

But there was one problem. He didn't have any sales experience. He didn't know anything about real estate or the sales process in general. Needless to say, he went months without any sales. He told me, "This is impossible. There are already so many brokers and they are much more efficient than me!"

I could see that his initial excitement for making a lot of money faded away. He was struggling to get even one sale. I encouraged him to keep going and arranged his meeting with one of my contacts who is a successful real estate broker.

They hit it off immediately. My contact agreed to help Naveen improve his overall sales strategy. Later, they even started working together.

After two years, I met Naveen again. He was like a new man. His posture was more upright. His handshake was firmer. His dressing style was sharper. His voice was calm and he looked me right in the eye. I could feel his confidence.

It was refreshing to see how much he had changed. I asked him what happened to his real estate sales business. He told me everything - how he had to learn new knowledge and skills, develop more confidence, become more proactive, face challenges daily, and work much harder.

His income was among the best real estate brokers in the city. He had achieved his goal. He became a successful real estate broker.

I asked jokingly, "What was the best part about your journey? A lot of money?"

He said, "No. I think the best part was all the bullsh*t I had to deal with. It forced me to push outside my comfort zone on a daily basis. It changed me. It changed my thinking. It changed my life."

He continued, "Even though I have a few more bucks to spend now, the way I had persevered through the obstacles - sometimes failing & sometimes winning at them - is my most proud memory."

"More than the money itself, I like who I have become. I now have the skills to make money anytime, anywhere. Now, I am confident that I would always be able to take care of myself and people close to me."

Naveen seemed quite happy and relaxed. Not because he made a lot of money, but because he became a person who *can* achieve his financial goals.

In the end, happiness is never about what you achieve. It is about making progress, facing challenges, and solving problems.

In the process of achieving your goals, you become a new person. You start becoming the best version of yourself. You start tapping into your true potential. You start using your natural talents - your gifts - and THAT is real, true happiness.

How to implement forward momentum in your daily life?

We just discussed how forward momentum - the flow of progress - creates true happiness, peace, and fulfillment.

But how do we apply it in our daily life?

Momentum is built by taking actions consistently. Let's look at a step-by-step process to implement forward momentum in your day.

Step #1: Decide your main goal

The first step is to decide what you want to accomplish. You cannot make progress if you don't have something to move towards. Define your goal.

Step #2: Break down the goal into smaller, more manageable tasks

If you are just starting out and want to build forward momentum, break down the large goal into a series of smaller steps. Smaller steps demand less effort from you. The less effort is required, the more work you do. The more work you do, the more momentum you gain.

For example, if you want to lose weight, start drinking green tea every morning instead of coffee and be persistent with that. After a few days, add 30 minutes of walk in your day. Soon after that, replace oily and fried food with green vegetables.

Take it easy in the beginning. Start small and do activities which require only little effort. Once you get comfortable, begin taking up challenges which demand more. For example - eat only healthy food, cut off all sugar and processed food, exercise regularly, strictly following your schedule, etc.

As you complete smaller challenges, you will start gaining momentum. It will become increasingly easier to take action regularly.

Step #3: Maintain your progress

As you keep taking action and complete more tasks, your momentum will get stronger. The more momentum you gain, the easier it will be to take even more action. Soon, you will reach a point where it will be easier to take more action than to stop.

This is the power of forward momentum.

And this will have a spill-over effect on all areas of your life. Momentum is energy, and by practicing it, you are putting energy in your everyday life. You will feel more alive and vibrant. The joy of taking down challenges, coupled with satisfaction from moving in the direction of your desires will create such a high, you will not want to stop.

At such a point, the forward momentum is really on your side. You will breeze past any obstacles & problems without giving a second thought. It's like shifting to the fast lane to success. Moving forward will become your default way of thinking and behaving.

But you have to be careful as well. Just as the momentum is gained by taking action, it can decrease or even die out if you stop. You have to keep taking action regularly to build and sustain healthy levels of momentum. Do not think once you gain momentum, it will continue on its own forever. If you stop, momentum will start decreasing, and with time, it will fade away.

So have both of these factors in mind - a) taking frequent action creates and sustains momentum. b) being stagnant will kill momentum.

Use this knowledge to your advantage and never lose your momentum. The higher your momentum, the stronger your actions. Stronger actions lead to growth, which leads to happiness and fulfillment.

"Happiness comes from progress. And progress shows up in the form of growth and contribution" - Tony Robbins

And remember, no matter how many mistakes you make or how slow you progress, you're still way ahead of everyone who isn't trying.

The relationship between action, purpose, and happiness

Taking action towards your purpose makes you grounded. It acts as an anchor that keeps you stable when the rest of things in life are going crazy. Sometimes, your mission, your purpose is the ONLY thing that keeps you sane.

You might be heartbroken, suffered huge financial loss, have health problems, but no matter how stressed you are due to the circumstances in life, you can always find happiness in your calling. Many times, having a mission or an objective is the only thing that keeps you going.

I cannot count how many times I was hurt emotionally, financially, or physically but I always found salvation in my mission. No matter how much it hurts inside, as soon as you start taking action... something magical happens.

You become completely present to the current moment. All worries, anxiety, fears, sadness, and despair start fading away and are replaced by a sense of peace and comfort. After a few of these kinds of experiences, you realize that you can always fall back on your mission whenever you face a crisis in life.

Your calling, your purpose, your mission will always be there, and it will make you realize that everything else in life in uncertain. The only thing that is certain is your mission and how you can depend on it to never leave you.

In real life, money comes and goes. Relationships come and go. Even your body will deteriorate. There is just one constant – your calling.

Nobody can take your purpose away from you. It cannot be stolen. It cannot be taken away. As long as we live, our mission will be there, providing us a sense of meaning and purpose in life.

That is why I believe that our calling originates from our higher self –the one that is connected to God (the universe if you may). Each one of us has been given a unique purpose, and it provides a context in the vast world full of uncertainty.

We do not know where we came from and where we go after death. What is life? What is death? Why was the world created? Everything is unknown.

The one thing that gives us even a remote context to this mystery called life is our calling. That is the one constant. That is the one thing we can depend on.

Once you discover it, your mission will be your life-long companion. You will learn to love it... and in return it will give you a sense of security, purpose, and happiness like nothing else can.

A true story: How a purpose beat cancer?

During a routine checkup, the doctor told a woman that she was suffering from lung cancer. It was in its starting stage and they would try everything out to cure it. She got admitted in the hospital and after three months of constant effort, the doctors gave up. They told her there was nothing that could be done.

The woman was devastated.

She had two small children, both boys, with no father.

She cried and pleaded profusely to the doctors, "Please do something. I have two kids. I cannot leave my children like this. They have nobody to take care of them."

The doctors tried to calm her down, but a mother's heart never calms down when it comes to safety of her children.

At night, in her dark room, she lay on her bed, with tears dripping down from her eyes, thinking about her children.

"What will happen to them?"

"Who will feed them when they get hungry?"

"Who will be there when they need something?"

"What if someone takes advantage of their innocence?"

She decided that she must live.

She closed her eyes and prayed, "God, I cannot leave like this. Please. Don't call me just yet. I have some responsibilities that are very important. I cannot come like this."

She made it a mission to live through the cancer.

She started imagining getting well and started talking as if she was getting better. Everyone saw that and felt sorry for her. They thought she was going crazy because there was nothing that could be done now.

One day, it was raining outside; the doctor came with a check-up report in his hand, feeling a bit too enthusiastic. He told her that cancer was not growing at the pace it did before. Her condition seemed to be getting stable.

Miracles do happen in this world.

She held that report with tears in her eyes and hope in her heart.

To everyone's astonishment and joy, she was released from the hospital a month later. She returned back to her home, to her children.

Years went by, her children graduated from college. The older one got in a marketing firm in a new city. The younger boy stayed with his mom and got a job as cashier in a local bank.

One month after her younger child got a job, she died... from her cancer.

Call it what you may... luck, chance, or miracle.

I believe it's an astonishing example of having a purpose.

After the world had given up hope, the only thing that kept her breathing through her cancerous lungs was her children.

That is the power of purpose. I believe everything is possible in this world if you dedicate yourself to a cause.

For her, it was her children.

What is yours?

CALCULATED INFLUENCE

Era of technology or era of distraction

"*Success at anything will always come down to this: focus and effort, and we control both.*" - Dwayne Johnson

Its morning and you just arrived at your desk, ready to get some work done, "Oh man, this is gonna be good." You turn on your PC or laptop and open up a fresh file. You know what needs to be done and how.

You start working and everything seems to be fine. Suddenly you start getting emails with 'urgent' in their subject line. You stop your work and go through that email. As soon as you respond to it, you receive five more emails.

Now, you seem to be losing your focus. You think, "I need a little more energy. Let's take a break!"

You open Facebook, 20 minutes fly by. You open YouTube, an hour disappears. You realize its lunchtime now. Half the day is gone and you haven't done any significant work.

How many times that has happened?

A study, sponsored by Hewlett-Packard, conducted in the UK found that the bombardment of emails, cell-phone calls and instant messages received by modern workers can reduce their IQ equivalent to losing a night's sleep or smoking marijuana.

"If left unchecked, info-mania' will damage a worker's performance by reducing their mental sharpness," according to Glenn Wilson, psychiatrist, University of London, UK.

Attention is the most valuable commodity in the market right now. Don't give it away for cheap. Top organizations know the importance of capturing the attention and focus of the masses. They all believe "where the attention goes, money follows" principle. It is disheartening to see that an average office worker doesn't realize it.

But to help us minimize distractions, several apps and productivity tools have been developed. Some apps provide a digital to-do list and track your progress. Another app blocks certain websites for a period of time. Another one tells you to take breaks in-between and yet another one for blocking you from accessing your inbox.

I am not kidding.

But they don't provide a permanent solution. All of these apps are located in your phone or computers... which are the two biggest sources of distractions in the first place. It's a digital solution to a digital problem which completely neglects the thought that you should be in control of your attention.

You should take control because focusing on one specific work or area of specialization provides incredible results. Look at Google. They are laser-focused on web-search. Look at Intel. Intel's main focus and the largest source of revenue are Microprocessors.

And it's not just large organizations. Undivided attention also leads to some of the biggest personal success stories in the world.

J.K. Rowling was completely absent from social media when writing her Harry Potter novels. Colonel Sanders started KFC just by working with one chicken recipe.

With the endless number of apps, advertisements, and devices specially designed to capture our attention, it became increasingly hard to maintain focus for any period of time. The people (or organizations), who master the skill of focused action earn success and wealth beyond their imagination.

Here's the good news - focus is a learnable skill. It takes effort and new strategies to deal with distractions, and it is definitely worth it. Anyone can learn to be more focused, centered, and mentally alert all day. And you can do it without taking any drugs or using any apps.

What is calculated influence?

As we go through our day, there are lots of things which demand our attention like urgent emails, calls, text messages, family responsibilities, hobbies, friends, etc.

As we get caught up in other work or chores, we tend to forget about our primary objective.

The human mind tends to put things in the background if it's not something which demands immediate attention. And because our primary goals usually require a period of time to accomplish, it tends to get 'out of focus' for the majority of the day. And it takes a lot of mental energy to switch back to the important tasks.

An effective way to minimize distractions and increase your focus is the principle of "calculated influence".

Whenever you have *free time*, immerse yourself in pictures, audio & information related to your main objective. Read books, watch videos, view pictures, read information about your chief goal.

For example, if your goal is to meet your sales target by the end of the month, watch sales videos on YouTube in your *free time*. If you looking to launch a new software in the target market, read customer reviews for similar software, go to different websites and read customer experiences, watch related videos on YouTube, read about its earlier versions and technical improvements.

Why do we need to do that?

Let's suppose you got up this morning feeling pumped up. You are very motivated and raring to go. But later during the day, you get caught up in some other work-related issue or maybe a friend needs your help.

It's very easy to forget about your main goal when you are juggling several things at once. It causes a loss in focus and worse, you start to get thoughts like - "oh I cannot focus on my goals for long. Maybe I am just not cut out for this kind of thing" or "I keep forgetting about my goals, maybe they are not so important for me?"

It takes a toll on your self-belief. Slowly but surely, your confidence starts going down.

The solution here is to *deliberately expose yourself* to your goal so you can see it, hear it, and read about it. It will make sure your goals are in your mind all the time - on and off the work.

Whenever you have some *free time*, instead of checking social media messages or watching random music videos, watch something related to your goal - any new information, review, people's opinions, how other successful people achieved it and so on.

It can be a video, book, blog, audiobook, pictures or anything else related to your goal. I call it - "calculated Influence"

Dwelling on your desire.

Immersing yourself in it.

But to clear things up, it does not mean that you should watch videos all day and not take action. Focused influence is meant to be done in *spare time*, in place of other unneeded activities we do when we get free.

For example, you want to grow your business and have scheduled marketing work from 11 am to 4 pm. Do not waste those precious five hours by reading an article about the luxurious lifestyle of big business owners.

When it's time to work, do your best work. When you get some free time to do other activities, you can choose to spend it reading/watching anything related to your main objective.

It's your answer against distractions and negative influences. That's another positive aspect of calculated influence. It protects you from indulging in some activity which may cause you to be distracted for the whole day. It guards your mind against other negative influences like gossiping, reading rumors, wasting time on social media because you are spending your free time focusing on your goal.

As you can imagine, deliberate exposure can boost your concentration, productivity, and motivation to a much higher level than before. In my own experience, it makes the mind completely focused on the goal. Later, regardless of the activity I'd be doing, my goals were always on my mind. I found it very effective. It truly made my focus stick to my primary objective all the time. The surge in my levels of motivation & concentration was amazing.

To recap:

1. When you are working, put your complete attention on doing the best work possible.

2. In your free time, you should be doing the following:

- Watch videos, movies, TV programs related to your goals.
- Listen to songs, audiobooks, and podcasts on your chosen objective.
- Read books, articles, news, and blogs to collect new information on your goals.
- Talk about it with open-minded people who support you and your cause.
- Create a vision board - a place where you keep different pictures of your goals.

Many people set a goal but do not focus on it frequently. Calculated influence will keep your goal at the forefront of your attention and ensure that the intensity of desire never fades away.

"Industry leaders concentrate single-mindedly on one thing - the most important thing, and they stay at it until it's complete." - Brian Tracy

MIND MATTERS

There were two brothers. Their father had a drinking problem. He used to bring a lot of alcohol home at the end of each day and drink in front of his sons. His health kept deteriorating. Eventually, he passed away.

Both of his sons grew up. One became a successful and wealthy man while the other became broke and had a drinking problem just like his father.

When people asked them how they became the way they are, the successful son replied, "I saw my father bring a lot of alcohol into the house and I decided to stay away from it and focus on developing good habits."

The broke son replied, "I saw my father bring a lot of alcohol into the house and it caused me to start drinking as well."

Both brothers had the exact situation growing up but one used it to his benefit while the other used it as an excuse to waste his life.

In their childhood, both brothers were similar in all aspects - age, education, height, fitness, etc. Then why their lives turned out to be so different? What was the reason behind such a drastic result in their lives?

They both had a different mindset.

An optimistic mind gives you power over your circumstances instead of circumstances having power over you. It's a little thing which makes a big difference. It's not what happens to you, but how you react to it that matters.

Positivity is a mental state that expects things to go well. It is a mental habit of believing that eventually things would happen and not entertaining negative thoughts and doubts for too long.

But it's not *only* about thinking. There is a *functional side* to it. You think about finding solutions to the problems and do your best to solve them. It is about taking action proactively. You take full responsibility for your life and face challenges as they come.

It's not a blind faith that things will turn out okay. You think about practical solutions and *carry them out* diligently.

Why do you think one person has an optimistic outlook, while the other dwells in negativity? Both may look quite similar in all aspects - education, age, culture, background, society, etc.

The difference is the mindset.

Whenever a positive person faces a challenge, his focus would be on finding a SOLUTION to the problem. It would be easy for him because he would imagine a bright future. He BELIEVES in a better future.

When a person with a negative mindset deals with similar challenges, he would ignore the possibility of sunshine behind the mountain. He would focus on the negative - how bad things are, it's taking too much time, it's not going to work and so on.

Even happiness is a mindset. We can make ourselves miserable, or happy & strong. The amount of effort is the same.

Everyone has the potential to live a fulfilling life. The difference lies in how we look at things. When someone views the world as a horrible place, he or she has taken themselves out of the game before they even had a shot at happiness.

Life is just too short to be gloomy all the time. If you cannot laugh at yourself, call me... I'll laugh at you. Then you laugh at me.

You cannot change other people, situations, weather, and the world. All you can change is yourself, but sometimes that alone changes everything.

The impact of a small change

The good news is, even a small shift in mindset can bring great results.

One of my friends used to struggle with being social in his office. He was an introvert by nature and had troubles opening up to new people. He always said, "I have nothing to talk about, and even if I did, they will not like me anyway." I sat down with him and convinced him to just say hello to people in his office and smile. He agreed because it was only a small shift in behavior.

The results were amazing. People were very receptive to his greetings and started conversations themselves. Initially, my friend was a bit nervous in conversations but it quickly became a habit. Now he is well known by his colleagues and has a reputation of a warm and social person.

A tiny shift in the mindset gave such a great result.

In life, success and failure are only inches apart. A very small shift is needed to get either result. No matter how many mistakes you make or how slow your progress is. You're still way ahead of everyone who isn't trying.

Cultivate a positive mindset.

If you want more proof, look at people who are consistently at the top of their respective field - CEOs, successful entrepreneurs, world-famous actors, award-winning athletes, great singers, artists and professionals who became icons of their generation - all have a positive mindset in life.

If you read the autobiographies of famous people, who are considered 'greats' of their field, the importance of attitude becomes apparent. Nelson Mandela, Steve Jobs, Albert Einstein, Mahatma Gandhi, Mother Teresa, and countless other great people's stories are proof that whatever your aim, a positive mindset will bring success and fulfillment, while negativity will lead to an inevitable downfall.

Your mindset determines your direction.

This is especially true nowadays. A positive mindset is very valuable. It gives you the resilience to face the harshness of life. You cannot always have a good day, but you can always face a bad day with positivity. No matter how big your problems get... if you look for the positive things in life, you'll find them.

The reverse is also true. Look around and you will find that negative people usually wind up being miserable their whole lives. They lack gratitude and general satisfaction. Their relationships become toxic and eventually get destroyed.

And because the mindset is contagious, you have to keep yourself away from negative people. We all have some negative, "emotional leech" type of people in our life. Each one of us knows a few, and it's best to keep your distance away from them as much as possible.

I have identified some people like that in my life and minimized my interactions with them. One of my friends introduced me to Raj. At first, I liked him, but later when I started hanging out with him, I realized he was constantly complaining about everything. He could find fault in everything & everyone. No matter how I tried to be normal around him, his strong negative outlook overwhelmed me every time.

Soon 'I' started pointing out faults in things, which I don't normally do. My other friends started telling me that I was changing. I was not positive and upbeat as before. Then I realized how strongly people influence each other. I minimized my interactions with Raj and decided to stay away from negative attitude as much as possible.

How to develop a positive mindset?

Be near positive people. Watch how they talk, what they say, how they think. Expose yourself to positive people as much as possible.

It is a psychological fact that we become a combination of five people with whom we spend most of our time. Be around people who are successful, positive, grateful and your mind will start adopting their behavior automatically. We subconsciously absorb the thinking of the other person, whether it is positive OR negative. That's the way our brains are wired.

"Associate yourself with people of good quality, for it is better to be alone than in bad company" - **Booker T. Washington**

What to do if you can't find positive people around you?

Don't be discouraged if you can't find positive people to hang out with. I discovered that great books, audio, video, programs, etc., all count towards changing your mind to be positive. It's not only about the surrounding people. It's about the top five "influences" that affect you on a daily basis.

Reading a book by someone who is massively successful will influence your mind to think like them. As you continually read, watch or listen to top individuals, you will gradually begin to adopt their beliefs and mindsets, which would be really helpful if you can't find people like that in your actual life.

One of the biggest advantages of having a positive mindset is that it changes your focus from "surviving" to "thriving". Have you noticed people who are just coping through life? Their whole motivation is to just "get by". For them, having just enough to survive is FINE.

With the right mindset, you will see situations and people differently. Your focus will be on what's good and what's possible. There will be aliveness inside you which other people will instantly notice. You will have more passion and zest for life because your dreams are ALIVE.

"Be the one thing you think you cannot do. Fail at it. Try again. Do better the second time. The only people who don't tumble at the high wire are those who never mount the high wire" - **Oprah Winfrey**

Imagine yourself on a boat in the middle of a lake. The boat is your mindset and the shores on either side are happiness and misery. If your mindset is right, you will move towards the shore of happiness. If you embrace negativity, you will move in the opposite direction, misery.

Some people ask me whether it is possible to change the course if you have been moving in the wrong direction. My answer: I firmly believe it's NEVER too late to change. You can always change at any point in your life.

There are countless examples of people who changed their destiny after the age of 50, 60, 70. It'll be a little tougher if you have been in a negative spiral all your life. But it is 100% POSSIBLE. Many people, exactly like you, have changed their life.

It's never too late...

21-day mindset challenge

This is a great way to develop a positive mindset. For the next 21 days, find *one* good thing in people you meet and the situations you are in. Just *one* is enough (but more is obviously better). If you find it hard, keep in mind that every bad situation will have something positive. Even a stopped clock shows the correct time TWICE a day.

Do your best at it. Around 21 days, it will become a habit.

Bonus step: Walk outside for 20 minutes

This is an optional step but it will speed up the change process. Go out for a 20-minute walk in fresh air for 21 days while doing the positive mindset challenge. If possible, try to get some sunshine by walking in the evening or early mornings. If you are already working out, you can skip this step.

Exercise releases *endorphins* and other "feel good" hormones in your brain. They make you feel happier and positive. If you are up for it, a simple 20-minute walk daily can really make a difference in how you feel.

In a research done by the Harvard institute, researchers have found that technical knowledge is only fifteen percent of achieving success. The rest of the eight-five percent comes from having a positive mindset and optimism.

Be an optimist because there is not much use of being anything else. A positive mindset will let you do everything better than negative one will.

I believe that sometimes the bad times in our lives put us on a direct path to the very best times of our life. Whenever you feel discouraged or depressed, try your best to change your mindset. Ships don't sink because of the water around them. They sink because of the water that gets *in* them. Don't let what's happening around you get inside you and weigh you down.

Happiness is not by chance, but by choice... and it's all in the mindset.

THE LAW OF LEAST EFFORT

"Depending on what they are, our habits will either make us or break us. We become what we repeatedly do" - Sean Covey

What is a habit?

Habits are our thoughts and behaviors that we indulge in repeatedly, without giving much thought to them. These are almost automatic. Research on human behavior shows that more than 70% of what we do in our day is unconscious. Means we do not think much about it. Typical present-day activity for a normal person resembles yesterday to a staggering amount.

We get up at nearly at the same time. Brush our teeth & take a shower. Get ready and go to the office by the same route that we do every day. Meet & greet the same people. Check our emails before work as usual. Go to the same place for lunch at a fixed time. Come back home through the same route. Talk with friends & family. Watch your favorite TV show.

There are only little variations in our day. And we tend to maintain our routine without giving it much thought.

Man is a creature of habit.

We never question why we are going to the office from this route. Why not try some other route? We could, but we don't. We talk to some people regularly. We don't ask ourselves why. Breaking our fixed routine feels uncomfortable.

When a habit gets old, it gets so ingrained in our mind that we stick to our routine even if a better, newer alternative exists now. We change old habits ONLY when it causes us lots of pain & stress. Otherwise, we tend to stick to our daily routine. That is the key to changing bad habits, but more on that later.

Types of habits

There are two types of habits – positive and negative. If a habit is beneficial for us, it is called a positive habit and if a habit is causing us more harm than good, that's a negative habit.

The idea is to get rid of our negative habits and replace them with positive ones.

Your habits have a massive amount of impact on the level of happiness & positivity you feel in day to day life. If you have a habit of sleeping very late at night, it makes you feel tired & sleepy all day the next day. If going to the gym in the morning is habitual for you, your body will get fitter and you will feel energized the whole day.

If someone spends their weekends in bars/clubs, drinking & using drugs to loosen up & feel high, it will wear their health down fast.

We all have several habits. Some are good. Some are bad. And the surprising fact about all of it is that we didn't consciously decide which habits we form. Most of the time, we start doing something just out of curiosity and soon it becomes a habit.

Now it feels so comfortable that we do not question whether we should do it or not. We just go ahead and do it.

We stop and think about changing a habit only when it will be causing us severe pain & distress. A person takes a puff of cigarettes because he wants to feel connected with his buddies. He wants to feel belonged. It always starts with a good intention. But pretty soon, he starts smoking 15 Marlboros a day.

He knows that smoking is very harmful to health, causes thousands of deaths every year but he does not quit.

Why?

Because smoking is not causing IMMEDIATE pain for him. His mind says "I will stop smoking from next month. It is not causing any harm right now."

Pleasure in the present always trumps over the pain in the future. Our brain is naturally wired to do whatever feels good at the present moment.

This natural tendency for immediate pleasure is what makes changing bad habits very difficult.

How habits are formed?

This is how habits form in a nutshell. In the human brain, there is a network of pathways and electrical signals called neurons pass through it. When we do an action or think about something, neurons pass through a fixed pathway unique to that specific thought or behavior.

As we continue to repeat that specific thought or action, more and more neurons pass through that mental pathway, making it bigger & stronger. The more you repeat a behavior, the more neurons pass through the mental pathway causing it to grow bigger and allow more neurons to pass through.

After some time, the mental pathway connected to that thought or behavior become so strong, it makes the flow of neurons much faster and easier, making the behavior effortless and thus, forming a habit.

That is a simple way to understand how habits are formed. The more we repeat a thought or behavior, the effortless it becomes... till a point where it becomes a habit.

After a habit is formed, it is very hard to change it. It has formed a strong neural pathway in the brain. You are biologically wired to that habit.

But with some help & effort, it is possible to replace it with a new habit.

It's not easy but it is certainly do-able. Older habits are even more difficult to change because they have been very deeply ingrained in our brain. It would take a lot of effort to replace a habit like that. But it is possible to change very old habits as well. It will take more effort but it will be worth it in the end.

The difference in the kind of life we desire and the life we have right now comes down to our habits. If we have a habit of eating healthy and exercising daily, our body will be fit & full of energy making us feel much better in everyday life.

A habit of reading books and implementing ideas contained in them creates a huge impact in several areas of life, especially finances. In the world of finance, knowledge is power. A habit of reading will go a long way in helping you figure out ways to expand your business and income.

Regular practice of meditation makes you calm & focused, increases your empathy and energizes your mind, turning you into better husband, father, friend, business partner and an overall better person.

"The quality of your life comes down to your daily rituals" – Anthony Robbins

How to change a habit?

When you want to change a bad habit, you cannot just stop it. You have to replace that bad habit with a good one. If you only stop doing a bad habit, there will be a space. You will feel a lack. And soon, after your willpower gets depleted, you will go back to your old habit.

Willpower can only carry you for so long. If you depend on sheer willpower to not do a bad habit, you will eventually crack.

Think of willpower like this. We have a fixed amount of will power reserve in a day. As we go about our daily routine and exercise, our will power for various activities like not drinking a coke, take greens instead burger at lunch, stop yourself from indulging in office gossips, your will power reserves get lower & lower.

Till the end of the day when you reach home, you are feeling tired and have exhausted nearly all of your will power. That is the reason we tend to give up at the end of the day. A tired person starts eating a bag of chips when she had decided to lose weight. A man who is trying to give up smoking is more likely to pick up a cigarette when he is feeling tired later during the day.

When you sleep, your mind recovers and you awake with renewed willpower reserves. That is why you feel much more in control early on in the day. You are more likely to go to the gym, resist smoking, put down the bag of chips at the start of your day.

But in this hectic lifestyle, we cannot depend on willpower to stop our bad habit. It gets depleted. We ran out of our willpower. One bag of chips or a bowl of ice cream can undo the entire day of healthy eating and exercise.

It may work for some people but changing a bad habit is just based on willpower never worked for me. I found a better way that uses no willpower and thus gives us more control over our habits. It is the simplest yet effective way to change habits. I call it - changing habits by *the law of least effort*.

How to change habits using the law of least effort?

Step 1: Identify your temptations

When you are trying to change a bad habit, the first thing you must do is to identify what your temptations are. What causes you to think about indulging in your bad habit? For example, if you want to quit smoking, figure out what causes you to want to smoke a cigarette.

For some people, the *urge* to smoke comes up when they are feeling stressed. Some people have developed a habit of smoking after they finish lunch. For some people, the *urge* to smoke may be associated with a fixed time during the day.

Only you can figure out what causes the *urge* to indulge in your bad habit. If you are trying to lose weight, maybe the *urge* to start snacking arises when you see a packet of chips in the kitchen.

There is always a subject of temptation, which causes you to feel the *urge* to partake in old bad habit. You must pay attention and identify the subject of your temptations. Only then we could do something to stop our bad habits.

Step 2: Remove all temptation from the environment

Once you have identified your temptations, DO NOT depend on willpower to resist the *urge*.

Assume that there is no such thing as willpower. It does not exist (for you).

Remove all the things from your home & office that creates the *urge* inside you and/or allows you to indulge in your bad habit. If you are trying to quit smoking, DO NOT KEEP cigarettes in your home or office. If you are trying to lose weight, throw away all the fatty, sugar-filled consumables from home.

Make changes in your environment that it becomes impossible to access anything which could lead to old bad habits. When you don't have access to the things that may harm you, there will be no pressure on you to use willpower to keep yourself away from it.

That is a very effective way to keep your bad habits away without using your willpower. And another benefit of this method is that it does not deplete your will power. You can use that willpower to resist temptations when you go to a different environment, like a mall.

Suppose you are trying to lose weight. When you go to a mall, you are surrounded by salty, fried, sweet foods that can undo days of your diet & exercise. IF you have followed the first part of this method, you would have removed every unhealthy food from your home and have some willpower in reserve as a result.

You can use that willpower to resist temptations in environments where you cannot remove things which help you indulge in bad habits.

This is the second step for changing a bad habit. Removing temptation from your environment eliminates the mental struggle to resist your bad habit and creates the foundation for a quick, lasting habit change.

Step 3: Replace the bad habit with a good one

When you stop a bad habit using the above two steps, it will create a void. You have some needs that were being fulfilled by your old bad habit, like smoking helps you cope up with stress, eating chips makes you feel good.

When you stop your old habit, there will be a space. You still have those needs that are waiting to be fulfilled. If you do not find an empowering, positive alternative that fulfills those needs, you will revert to your bad habits.

Their needs are there and old habits were helping you fulfill those needs. You cannot just stop. The needs will make you go back. It is of vital importance that you find a positive habit that fulfills your needs without impacting your life badly.

Make sure the alternative, positive habit is as intense as your old bad habit. Which means the positive habit should provide you with all the good emotions that old habit used to give.

For example, if smoking helped you cope up with stress, replace smoking with the practice of deep breathing or meditation. It will make you even more efficient in a deal with stress than smoking. And when you combine the above two steps; temptation removal with adopting a good habit that fulfills your needs, you will kick your bad habits for good.

Keep doing this for 21 days. It takes around 21 days for the brain to rewire itself and make the habit permanent.

Additional step: Above three steps for changing bad habits is the MOST effective method I have found to change bad habits (and I have read countless books on the topic), but sometimes it may take one more step.

You must write down your reasons to why you want to quit your bad habits every day. Take a pen and paper, write down at least 10 reasons why you want to change. What your bad habits are costing you right now? What do you absolutely detest about your bad habit and why you MUST change it RIGHT NOW!

Make it emotional. Emotions create a deep impact on your motivation. Make sure the reasons that you write move you emotionally. If you only write sentences without any emotional significance, then it will be of no use.

Your 10+ reasons will build up some much disgust towards your bad habit that you will kick yourself for indulging in it and do whatever it takes to change.

Do not underestimate the significance of this little step. It will increase the potency of the above three steps several folds. I have used this step to change very old bad habits that I thought I could never change. I have changed habits that I thought became a part of my individuality.

For example, during college time, I was addicted to video games. It was really hurting my studies. I used to spend all my study time to play video games. Afterward, I would beat myself over it but again start playing as soon as I get back from college.

My friends said "It's no big deal, man. Everybody loves games. You are just stressing out over nothing."

But I knew something is very bad about this situation. I am spending so much money and time to study in college and I am wasting everything by playing a video game.

I read several books on habit change and experimented with the ideas. Soon, I found the combination of these three steps to be the most effective.

My temptation was "free time." Video games gave me a comfortable means to feel good whenever I had some time. There was no apparent downside and it gave goody-goody feelings. It soon became a habit.

Next, I uninstalled all the games on my PC and deleted all the online gaming accounts I had. If I wanted to install games, I would have to pay full price again and it would take 15 hours of downloading to install games again. I made it very difficult to play games again.

Third and the last step, I replaced my gaming habit with going out and socializing with people in my free time. I found spending time with friends and/or meeting new people gave me good emotions as much as video games.

After a month, I never even thought about playing video games. I graduated from my college with good performance in all subjects.

I stand by this whole process of habit change. In my personal experience, this is the best method I have come across and I have seen several.

Summary:

To change a habit by using the law of least effort, do the following:

- Identify what creates an *urge* inside you to indulge in your bad habit.
- Remove all objects from your environment which create the *urge*.
- Make it impossible for you to indulge in your bad habit by removing everything *related* to the bad habit from your environment.
- To make the change permanent, replace the old habit with a new habit. Make sure your new habit fulfills your needs like your old habit.
- Keep doing this for 21 days. It takes around 21 days for the brain to rewire itself and make the habit permanent.

THE COMMUNITY ADVANTAGE

The researchers at Harvard conducted one of the longest-running studies on "what makes a good life"? They followed the lives of 268 men from when they entered college in the 1930s till now. And after analyzing the whole lives of people, one thing came up as the biggest factor for living a happy, fulfilled life. And that one factor is - *our relationships with other people.*

(Study link: www.adultdevelopmentstudy.org)

Findings of the study suggest that it is by far the biggest determinant of happiness in the life of an individual. In the summer of 2009, psychologist George Vaillant said, "after working for 40 years on this study, I could sum up the entire happiness phenomenon in one word - Love"

(Study link: www.yuruuniverse.com/wp-content/uploads/2014/12/happiness-is-love.pdf)

Social connections and happiness

In life, nothing is certain. We are living in a world full of uncertainty. Whether that's good or bad, depends on how we look at it.

People fear the unknown when they expect the worst. At the time of crisis, we tend to go back in our shell. We prefer solitude. We believe being alone will make us focused so we can come up with solutions to our problems or get over grief.

Entrepreneurs, small business owners and people working in IT industry tend to be most prone to it. We think solitude will give us strength and focus. While it may work sometimes, there is a superior way to deal with challenges and setbacks.

Rather than facing the emotional burden alone, connect with other people who support you. There is a simple reason behind it - when you connect with others in your community, it magnifies your intelligence, courage, determination, motivation, and lightens your emotional burden.

Remember a time when you were really upset or sad over something and suddenly a friend or a family member came and took you outside (to some other place). You shared your problem with him or her, and after a few moments, you started feeling a LOT lighter. It was like suddenly a huge burden was removed from your shoulders. Now you were able to think more rationally about the problem.

This is the principle of *community advantage*. Our relationships and contacts are our biggest strength, whether we realize it or not. When you connect with people in your community, it instantly boosts you up in several ways. The more connected you are with your tribe (people who care about you), the happier you are.

Social connections and health

According to another study conducted by Lisa Berkman, Yale University School of Medicine, Connecticut, links the health of an individual to his or her social connections. Research findings state, "People who lack ties that provide for intimacy, a sense of belonging, opportunities for nurturance, and reassurance of worth are *physiologically stressed*. (Lack of) Social networks may indeed influence generalized susceptibility to illness."

(Study Link: www.annualreviews.org/doi/pdf/10.1146/annurev.pu.05.050184.002213)

Strong social connections reduce cortisol, the stress hormone, in the body and make us feel relaxed and happier. It may lead to optimal blood pressure and reduced risk of heart attack, thus prolonging the life expectancy of a person.

On the other hand, a lack of social connections has a detrimental effect on our health and mortality.

There is enough proof of the fact that strong relationships are crucial for our mental and physical health. The richer our social life is, the better we would feel and perform.

But then the question becomes - how to create new social connections and how to improve the relationships we already have in our lives?

If you already have good social skills and are enjoying the benefits of having strong bonds with other people in your life... Great, keep it up. But what if you are not socially well-adept? What can you do to deepen your existing relationships and form new alliances?

Let's look at some practical ways to create and improve our social relationships.

Practical ways to improve your social life (or how to connect with others as a shy introvert)

1. Express what's on your mind

As an individual, you have the right to fully express your thoughts, feelings, needs & wants to others. It's called being expressive.

Many people shy away from expressing their real thoughts. This leads to a lot of friction in their relationships. If we don't speak up and clearly state our intentions, we will never be understood by others.

Have you ever heard someone say - "Nobody understands me" or "Nobody cares about me"? All such problems stem from not willing to express yourself. Other people do not have psychic powers. They cannot read your mind.

Even people who have been with you for a long time need you to express yourself... because over time, your thoughts, needs, and wants change.

These changes may not be apparent to you, but they are to others. This creates misunderstanding, conflict, separation, divorce and every other friction in relationships known to mankind.

Speak your mind. Start expressing yourself. Let people know who you are and what you feel. That's the only way they can *clearly* understand you. It may seem like common sense, but in reality, many people are unable to open themselves up to others.

People are afraid of being rejected, disliked. They think if they express their desire, people would think they are greedy and selfish.

In reality, it's the other way round.

Being assertive and expressing, you will smoothen your relationships. It will make people understand you better, and will also motivate them to express THEIR needs as well. Things will be clear and every person will get a better chance to be understood. It's a win-win for all involved.

And speaking of win-win...

2. Think win-win

Whenever you are dealing with people, try to meet the needs of everyone involved. Final outcomes don't need to favor any one particular side. Try to make results beneficial for everyone. For example, your boss wants you to work overtime to finish the project early but you have other commitments. On the surface, both of your interests appear to be clashing with each other, but it's possible to turn it into a WIN-WIN situation.

One of many possible solutions could be: you could make an agreement with your boss to work on weekends as it will let you fulfill your commitments during the week and finish the project on time as well.

Try your best to make situation win-win for all. If your intent is positive, it will come across and people will respect you for it.

Make it a habit. Look for ways to create a win-win situation every time you can. The most admired leaders have this quality.

They have an image of 'solution-finders' and gained the trust of millions of people.

This is such a rare & desirable quality that if you can create a reputation for creating win-win situations, people will try to connect with you and even put you in leadership roles. We all want someone in authority who can produce outcomes favorable for all concerned parties.

It makes everybody feel safe with you. They would realize that they are under a capable authority which will never compromise their situation.

It's a great habit that will get you a lot of friends and connections. Another benefit of making a win-win situation is the amazing satisfaction you get afterward. Nobody is left wanting. No conflicts. You have added value to each side by fulfilling their needs. You are truly making the world a better place for everyone.

3. Winning respect and friendships

To create a win-win situation, you need to *understand* people and their needs. The best way to do it is by listening.

It's sad that in today's hectic world, where everyone is short on time, we have lost touch with our ability to truly listen. We want everything to be as fast as possible. Nobody has time to stop and listen.

People forget that listening to the other person is still the fastest way to win friends and make contacts. Listening does two important things: it makes the other person feel respected and you're able to understand them better.

In our 'attention-deficit' society, we all crave someone who listens to what we have to say. It makes us feel valuable and respected. Let's take an example - who is your best friend?

Your best friend is likely someone who listens to you, doesn't interrupt, and laughs at your jokes. We are very attracted to people who listen to us. Good listeners have an infinite supply of friends. People like spending time with them and end up introducing them to their friends.

It's one of the fastest ways to expand your social network. And for that, you need to know how to BECOME a good listener.

How to improve your listening skills?

a) Make frequent eye contact. Avoiding eye contact will make others think you are not interested in what they have to say.

b) Fully focus on the conversation. No excessive thinking or worrying. No scanning of the environment. Just put all your attention on the words being said.

c) Try to understand the real meaning or "gist" behind the words. Look at their facial expression, tone, and emotions. What is the real message they want to convey?

d) Give appropriate responses. Nod your head. Say "um-hm". Change your facial expressions. Basically, *act* like a good listener. People need your responses to continue talking. If you just stare blankly at the speaker, they would think you are not listening (or not interested in their topic).

Practice good listening in every conversation. Get good at it. This single skill will boost your social persona and likability to unprecedented heights.

4. Show your real self

Always be real. Show your true personality. Express your real thoughts and feelings. Many people don't because it's scary. You could get rejected. It takes courage to be yourself when the whole world is watching you.

People hide their true personality. They keep quiet and say only 'socially accepted' things. This is called 'creating a shell' around ourselves. Some people never come out of their shell. They keep hiding their true self from the outside world.

Life is just too short to live like this.

Instead, express your true self. Let the world know who you are and what you stand for. Maybe some people will hate you, but the majority will like and respect you for it. Everyone knows it takes courage to put your real personality on the line. You are basically exposing yourself to possible rejections. It takes guts.

When you open up, people notice. We live in a stifled society where people prefer to remain quiet and closed. When someone takes a stand for who they are and express their true self, it's very attractive. We find it addictive to watch. For example, look at celebrities.

Celebrities are people who can express themselves fully even when they are under the spotlight. They openly show their personality even when the world's attention is on them. They realize some people won't like them for who they are... but it still doesn't stop them from being themselves. This universally attractive quality eventually win them the admiration of millions of people worldwide.

It takes courage and practice, but in the end, well worth it. Your experience of life would be richer and more satisfying. You will come across as a genuine, confident individual who inspires people to break out of their own shell.

5. Appear friendly by smiling more

A smile symbolizes happiness and positivity. When you meet someone and smile, it shows you like and approve them. A genuine smile is irresistible. Studies have shown that every culture in the world associate a smile with happiness and acceptance, no matter what language they have.

It means the same thing to an American, Japanese, African, French, Australian, Indian and for every other person in the world. Smile is truly a universal 'language'.

It adds positivity to your interactions, makes people feel good, and goes a long way in creating a positive first impression.

How to charm them with your smile?

When you meet someone, look at them, and THEN smile. It creates magic. When you make eye contact 'before' smiling, the other person will think you have analyzed them and then approved their persona with a smile.

It will really make them warm and friendly towards you because we tend to like people who like & approve us.

So, make eye contact, and then smile.

Make sure your smile appears genuine. There are two things which make a smile genuine:

a) In a genuine smile, the corners of your eyes (crow's feet) are wrinkled. Imagine 'smiling with your eyes'.

b) Your teeth should be visible. A genuine smile has visible teethes. But use your judgment. See your smile in a mirror. If you look better with closed lips then keep it that way.

Practice both elements of a smile in a mirror. It's very easy. Pretty soon you will be charming your acquaintances with an irresistible smile.

21 Day challenge: become more friendly

Here is a 21-day challenge to make improve your social life and happiness.

Smile at 5 living, breathing creatures every day for 21 days. They can be your family members, friends, co-workers, counter clerks, neighbors, pets, birds, or any living creature. You have to look at them and give a genuine smile.

Five smiles every day for 21 days.

Bonus step: You can go one step further and look for opportunities to help other people. When you find someone who needs a helping hand, give it to them. For example, help an old lady cross the street. If somebody dropped their stuff on the ground, help them to pick it up. If somebody is in a hurry, give them space to go ahead. Give small tips to homeless people. When you help other people, you prove to yourself that you're a helpful, friendly person. Along with giving you immense joy, being a helpful person will boost your social life by unbelievable proportions.

Tip: You can mix it with the previous 21-day challenges if you like. You can do them all together. For example, do a 5-minute gratitude morning exercise, followed by a 20-minute walk in the park, and smile at 5 people (or pets or birds) as you go about your day.

Doing these exercises together will give you even faster results.

DISORDER MANAGEMENT

"Life is a series of natural and spontaneous changes. Don't resist them - that only creates sorrow. Let reality be reality. Let things flow naturally forward in whatever way they like." - Lao Tzu

People are afraid to fail. Many give up even before they take the first step. Thoughts like "What's the use?", "Why try? I will never get that", "It's beyond my abilities" and "I have never achieved something like this before"; race through their minds every time they go after a BIG goal.

It's very common to experience thoughts like that. All people experience fear and doubts, especially when they go for a goal which is beyond their past achievements.

But what if I tell you that you can ENSURE your success & happiness one hundred percent, and there is no such thing as a failure?

Let me introduce you to the principle of disorder management.

Disorder management

Disorder management represents the idea of *making changes* in business and personal life in order to make further progress. It's the way to manage chaos at work or home.

Contrary to what people may believe, failure is not the end of the road to success. Failure is an indicator that you need to try something different to obtain your goal. You need to change your approach, do something different if your current plan is not working, and keep trying out different approaches/plans/actions until you find something which works.

Let's suppose you are trying to get in shape. You're going to the gym six times a week and following a healthy diet plan, but still not able to lose weight. Instead of getting disheartened, collect more information - consult your dietitian, read the best books on weight loss, etc.

Find out how the human body works, how we put on fat and how fat is converted into energy. Find out different forms of exercises like high-intensity interval training, cross-fit, etc. New information would show you several different ways to lose weight.

Pick any one. Make changes in your diet and exercise routine and continue it for a month or two. Look for the progress. If you don't see any improvement, make changes in your diet and exercise program yet again.

Stick to it, and look for the results. Rinse and repeat until you find a diet & exercise plan which works for you.

Success is virtually GUARANTEED if you keep trying different approaches to obtain your objective. The ONLY way you cannot succeed, is when you CHOOSE to stop trying.

Success is like finding a combination of a lock. You may need to try a few different combinations, but if you persist, you'll eventually get the lock open. Persistence, when combined with changing your approach, is the recipe for guaranteed success.

Some people may ask, "But how do I find other approach options? How would I know what to try next?"

We live in an age where information is available at every moment. There are thousands of books, eBooks, YouTube videos, seminars, audiobooks, blogs, newsletters, CD and DVD programs, podcasts and other sources available to you right now. Take advantage of them.

Most successful people in the world are constant learners. They never stop learning. Bill Gates was a college dropout who became one of the richest people in the world. He attributes the majority of his success to being a constant learner.

Research repeatedly shows that learning and constantly improving yourself are much more powerful predictors of success than a college degree. While it's great to have a college degree, you need to become a student for life.

When you learn, you grow. When you think you've made it and stop learning, it all starts going downhill.

Anthony Robbins said, "*In this world, nothing is constant. Either you are growing or dying.*" Try to keep educating yourself. You can find people who have accomplished a lot but are still learning new things every day.

Whatever your challenges may be, if you look for a solution, you will find it. Look around, it blows my mind that we can get millions of dollars' worth of information in a $10 soft-cover book!

Incredibly successful people, who have spent their lifetime overcoming challenges, wrote all their knowledge and experience in a little book... and you have access to it! You are fortunate enough to learn what they learned in about a fraction of the time it took them to discover all these solutions.

We are blessed to live in times like this. Think about it. You have a massive advantage over previous generations which didn't have the kinds of resources available to you now.

When you use this knowledge, you would discover several options to reach your destination. Pick any one, and start taking action. Look for progress and make changes if required.

Each individual who became successful had to embrace the principle of disorder management. Whether they had to change their attitude, behavior, plans, action, team or something similar, it's the "change" that ultimately brought them success.

I attribute 90% of my success to persistence and accepting change. Success never came easy for me. I always had to work harder than most people to achieve results.

At first, I used to get frustrated about it. "Why do I have to work extra hard?" I would often ask myself, "Other people seem to get by with much less effort."

But my struggles turned out to be a blessing in disguise. It forced me to analyze what I was doing wrong and learn the principles of happiness and success. I spent many years studying happiness and created a blueprint that can be applied by anyone to become happier and more successful. You have that blueprint in your hands right now.

Later, I realized that I can use this knowledge to help other people overcome their challenges as well thus, it led to the creation of my blog and books.

Charles Darwin revealed out that species which are unable to adapt to constant change are likely to be weeded out of existence. This adaptation – change – is even more important now because our society is changing and evolving at a rapid pace.

In this day & age, businesses as well as individuals, have to change constantly to keep up with the pace of technological evolution. Those who fail, become "extinct". Successful businesses go down, people lose their wealth, top athletes get kicked out of the competition - all because they failed to change.

On the other hand, people and businesses who DO adapt themselves to the current situation become leaders of their chosen fields. Think about the most successful individuals and corporations. Can you count how many times they had to change in order to make progress?

The popular wisdom of *'don't quit'* may not be enough anymore. Even if you keep going, you're still in danger of doing the same old thing over and over again. It's like beating a dead horse.

You must combine *'don't quit'* ideology with disorder management, and accept the fact that change is required to become wildly successful and happier in life.

Do not quit + make changes = success is guaranteed

In the past, I too fell in the trap of doing things repeatedly which didn't work, while expecting a different result. As if a magic fairy would appear and say, "Poor soul, you've worked hard enough. Let me give you what you want."

In life, success will never come from doing the WRONG things, no matter how persistent or hard-working you may be.

But when you combine persistence with the willingness to change... boom!

You will succeed.

Every time.

Failure is your guide

Whenever you achieve any result, it's a kind of feedback – either negative or positive. Positive feedback indicates, "You are going in the right direction. Keep going."

Negative feedback – failure or setback – represents, "Stop. Something is not right. It needs correction."

Always remember: when you experience failure, there is nothing to be ashamed of. You did your best at the time. Let it go and move forward. It may not feel good, but failure plays an important part in achieving success. Successful people are willing to fail more than other people to succeed.

"*I have missed more than 9,000 shots in my career. I have lost almost 300 games. 26 times, I have been trusted to take the game-winning shot and missed. I have failed over and over again in my life. And that is why I succeed.*" **– Michael Jordan**, basketball legend.

Any feedback, whether it FEELS good or not, contains very valuable information. It indicates if you are on the right course or not. It also highlights the need to make necessary adjustments in your plans & activities required to move forward.

Think of negative feedback (a.k.a. failure) as a clue. Instead of quitting, look at what isn't working and change it. Embrace change to such an extent that you are CONSTANTLY SEEKING feedback.

Once you start collecting feedback quickly and make the necessary corrections, you'll progress at a rapid pace. All the underlying issues will surface quickly and be dealt with. This constant refinement will make your process much smoother and efficient. You will be cruising towards success, both personally and professionally.

"Failing forward is the ability to get back up after you have been knocked down, learn from your mistake, and move forward in a better direction." **– John C. Maxwell**, success coach.

Now, instead of being afraid of failure, think of it as feedback and a necessary component of success. Every successful person had to go through challenges and failure, but they looked at it as an opportunity. You must too.

Remove the whole concept of failure from your mind. There is no such thing as failure. There is only feedback.

The ONLY way you cannot succeed... is when you stop trying.

Keep moving and you will reach your destination... every time.

It's a very liberating feeling. How would you feel when you know you cannot fail, EVER? What would you achieve? What kind of goals would you go for?

PART II

RECHARGE YOUR EMOTIONAL ENERGY

When we talk about energy, we normally talk about physical energy: "I am feeling tired," "I should take a nap," "Let's sit down for a minute." Things like that are meant to relax and recharge the energy of our body.

What if I told you that there is another kid of energy that needs recharging at multiple times in a day, especially if you are doing something which is using your mental horse power – and this energy is equally or more important than physical energy.

I like to call it "emotional energy." It is the energy for the mind.

Have you felt mental fatigue at any time during work even if you could go on physically? Have you ever found you mind too tired to do something, like writing or solving a puzzle? Have you sometimes found that you are unable to focus on an activity?

That is all caused by depletion of emotional energy. Not physical energy.

I discovered emotional energy while writing my first two books. Writing is very taxing on your mind. It takes a lot of brain processing power. When I was in a process of writing, I found that I frequently burned out mentally even when I had enough physical energy to sit and write more.

My body had enough juice to continue sitting and doing work, but I wasn't able to write. My brain just gave up after an hour or so of writing.

I thought that if I lay down for few minutes to rest and recharge my body, I would be able to work again.

I lay down on my bed and turned on the TV. After fifteen minutes, I felt rested enough. I had lots of energy because I eat healthy and exercised regularly.

But when I start writing again, I couldn't get my mind to put down letters on the paper. Nope. Still couldn't write. I took rest for an hour thinking that my body needed some more rest.

But that didn't help either.

My mind was still unable to come up with ideas and concepts that were even remotely interesting. If I forced myself to write, the quality went down tremendously and it felt as bad as hell.

I thought maybe I just naturally had a very low writing capacity and couldn't write more than 1000 words max.

I tried many different things to improve it.

Later I discovered that I was able to write more if I listened to my favorite songs for 10-15 minutes. Somehow it increased the quality AND quantity of my writing. I wasn't feeling as mentally burned out as before. I could write more WITHOUT taking hours of rest in between writing sessions.

As curious as I am, I started looking into this more and more. I found that energy of the mind is different than energy of the body. And the processes that relax the body are not as efficient in recharging the mind. These are two different processes.

Sleeping eight hours at night recharges both body and mind, but if we need to do mentally complex work for several hours a day, emotional energy and its rejuvenation is the key.

Emotional energy is the energy used by the mind. Notice how I didn't just call it mental energy. There is a reason for that.

The mind uses emotions to recharge itself.

Yes. A quick nap also helps, but not to the same extent.

AND emotional energy has a HUGE impact on the amount of happiness and joy we experience in our day. There is a difference of NIGHT and DAY between going through our day with enough emotional energy or without it.

Now, does that sound pretty important?

It is!

I have no idea why such an important part of our daily life has been neglected until now and why nobody talks about it.

Effect of emotional energy on your social life and happiness

I had a full-time day job AND was trying to write two books back to back. It was mentally exhausting. My mind used to be completely burned out. I felt tired all the time. But it wasn't physical, because I could go for walks of 30-40 minutes.

So it was clearly not about physical exhaustion. It was more related to writing or doing any creative task. My mind protested! I couldn't get myself to write. If I forced myself, the text came out rubbish.

Mental exhaustion also made an impact on the other areas of my life. It was hard to have a pleasant meeting with other people and maintain a conversation. Speaking and listening require mental energy and when you are running on empty – because of mentally taxing work – it makes every conversation feel like a chore.

Even more upsetting was if somebody made a joke and everybody else laughed, I just stared. I knew it was a good joke but I could not generate enough emotions inside to laugh out loud. I just wanted to get out of conversation and be alone. Being social was difficult. I didn't want to come across as a duck with no emotions and energy.

Avoiding social interactions was a safe way to go about the day.

However, the times I was alone were not that exciting either. It was hard to feel happy or enthusiastic about something. There was a constant urge to go lie down on sofa and watch TV to numb myself.

Watching TV was easy. I didn't have to think. I could just shut myself down and watch TV until it was time to sleep. I didn't have much energy to do anything else.

The turning point came when I decided to find ways to increase my writing capacity because, at the rate I was going, it would take more than a year to finish, and I didn't want that.

I started paying attention to everything I was doing in my day. There was one thing that came up and gave me a sliver of hope.

When I listened to few of my favorite songs, I felt something. It was like life was coming back in me. My mind felt a little, dare I say, alert.

That was the only time I felt something. It was not much, but it was the only clue I had at the time. I decided to find out more about it. I made a separate list of my favorite songs in my cell phone and listened to them for 30 minutes straight.

Afterwards, I felt somewhat better. It was not much improvement, but definitely better than before. I decided to delve deeper. I separated my favorite songs by the kind of emotions they summon inside. Some were sad songs, some were romantic, some were heavy metal... I like many different kinds of music.

I lay down on my bed and listened to my sad song collection first. Within 30 minutes, I was completely wrapped up in emotions generated by songs. It felt better but not by much. I was still feeling tired.

It was the same with romantic music. I felt better but not by that much.

The moment came after I put on happy, uplifting music. After just 15 minutes of positive, uplifting music, I got up completely refreshed!!

And it was not just a little difference. I got up COMPLETELY refreshed.

It was like a MIRACLE for me. If you don't have the kind of life where you live completely mentally exhausted, you could never imagine how crazy good I felt after I discovered this.

My work (and life) depended greatly on mental energy and I found a way to recharge it... in little as 15-20 minutes.

I was ecstatic!

From that day, whenever I felt mental exhaustion, I just lay down on my bed and rocked my favorite uplifting music. It worked like a charm for me every time.

How much of a difference did it make, you ask?

Well, I used to give up after writing around 1000 words in a day, now I was able to write 5000-6000 words in one day!

It was an unbelievable jump in both quality and quantity.

I felt a lot better during my day job. I was able to focus more on the tasks I did and was able to join conversations with my colleagues. Everybody started noticing the change in me. My friend asked me if I started taking any supplements.

People wanted to know what changed. How did I become so vibrant and enthusiastic all of a sudden?

I felt it too – the change – and it was not because of any multivitamins.

I am going to share my entire experience with emotional energy with you. We are going to cover everything about this vital yet unlooked aspect of our daily life.

Benefits of emotional energy

Having high emotional energy provides the following benefits:

1. It rejuvenates your mind.

2. It allows you to perform mentally taxing work like writing, solving a puzzle, or any creative work really.

3. It greatly increases the amount of happiness and enthusiasm you feel during your day.

4. It makes you emotionally resistant to negativity and setbacks.

5. It has the potential to double the amount of work that you do in a day (especially if it is mentally challenging).

6. You will be more social and meet people with more energy and enthusiasm.

7. It lowers your anxiety and self-consciousness.

8. It reduces the intensity of negative thoughts we all get during the day.

9. It increases your self-control throughout the day.

10. It has a big positive impact on the quality (and quantity) of any mind-related activities we perform during the day.

Lack of emotional energy:

1. Leaves you feeling mentally exhausted.

2. Makes you unable to perform mentally demanding tasks and creative works.

3. Slows down your thinking and imagination.

4. Makes you feel numb to emotions; feeling and expressing emotions (like laughter) becomes harder.

5. Causes you to become prone to procrastination and laziness.

6. Makes social interactions feel like a chore; you feel like dragging behind.

7. Decreases motivation and enthusiasm.

8. Creates the urge to avoid any work that demands thinking and attention.

9. Lowers the quality of work produced.

10. Causes feelings of being down and out, drained and/or overwhelmed.

How to recharge your emotional energy?

Now we come to the most important part in all of this – How to rejuvenate your emotional energy when you feel exhausted.

After two years of experimenting, I found that there are two main methods to replenish your emotional energy.

1. Generate emotions of happiness

Your emotional energy recharges every time you feel happy. Songs are an amazing way to generate feeling of happiness without much effort. I found that when I listened to happy, uplifting music, I instantly felt rejuvenated. After 15-20 minutes of music, I can continue mentally demanding tasks that I would have left alone for the day.

It is just not about music. Everybody is different. You may feel the same amount of happiness and joy by playing with your pets, taking a walk in the park, or talking to a loved one.

That is why I called this method "emotions of happiness" and not "listen to happy music."

It is not about songs. It is about any way you can generate feelings of happiness inside yourself. Any method you choose is fine as long as it makes you very happy.

Songs work the best for me. One of my friend's feels equally joyful talking to his girlfriend on phone. Another friend feels amazing by doing physical exercise. One watches comedy videos on YouTube and laughs out loud the whole time.

For me, even a forced laugh for one minute works wonders.

Everybody is different. You have to find your own way to make yourself feel happy. When you feel happy and excited, it brings out the emotions that get buried when we feel mentally exhausted. We feel energized, rejuvenated. A new life forms within us. We feel alive and vibrant. We feel like we can handle anything now.

2. Switching off the thoughts

Another way to feel mentally rejuvenated is by shutting down your thoughts. This can either be done through 15 minutes of meditation or taking a 15-minute long nap.

When we are emotionally exhausted, constant thinking keeps on draining the mind and prevents any replenishment. This is especially important if many of your thoughts are negative in nature. For example, if you are afraid or worried, your mind cannot replenish itself.

You must shut down the thinking process completely for some time by meditation or a quick nap. Even if you don't have any experience in meditation or napping, you might want to try these out. Both of these shut down constant thinking and allow the mind to recover the lost energy.

Watching TV serials or checking your friend's status on Facebook does not count as mind relaxation activities. Such activities drain out your energy rather than replenish it. Think about it. Do you remember the last time you watched TV for three hours, how did you feel afterwards? Were you full of energy and enthusiasm? Or feeling dull and more exhausted than earlier?

When you are exhausted, you have to shut down mental thoughts completely for some time, and that can only be done through sleep or meditation.

When I feel mentally exhausted after a long work session, I meditate for 15 minutes and it feels like somebody gave a shot of mental energy. I feel much better. It's the same with 15-minute naps. They rejuvenate physical and mental energy like there is no tomorrow!

UPDATE: Physical energy is also important. If you have a lot of emotional energy but lack physical energy, you will not feel as vibrant. The key is to keep both physical and emotional energy at higher levels.

Some everyday activities that consume a lot of emotional and physical energy:

1. Sitting in a chair for more than 25 minutes.

This is huge. Sitting does not come naturally for us. Human bodies were primarily designed to stand up and lie down. Sitting down on chair for long periods of time makes you feel drained. That's why nearly everyone sitting in an office depends on coffee to feel energetic.

Tip: Try to get up from your seat every 20-25 minutes.

2. Mentally demanding work like writing, designing, or solving a problem.

Mentally challenging tasks use a lot of mental energy. You start something and within minutes you can feel your energy draining. After an hour or so of heavy mental activities, you feel completely drained and are unable to go further.

You must take time to recharge whenever you feel that you cannot continue any longer.

3. Complaining, gossips and negative conversations.

Any negative talk, including complaining, gossiping, arguing, and put downs, makes you feel emotionally drained. Just as positive emotions like happiness and joy recharge your emotional energy, negative emotions drain you.

Even if you are not the one doing the complaining, participating in that sort of conversation depletes your emotional energy. Avoid negative people and conversations as much as you can.

4. Wasting your time.

Surprise!

If you have something important to do but you are procrastinating, that can be very damaging to your emotional energy. Do you remember the last time you had something to do and you went ahead and did it, even if you did not feel like doing it?

How did it feel, doing the right thing?

It always feels amazing to do what you know is important for you. It recharges your mind and body and fills you up with a sense of vibrancy. When you know there is an important project you must complete but you waste your time by watching TV and online videos, it takes a toll on your energy levels.

The more you procrastinate, the worse you feel and the harder it becomes to get yourself to do the work required. Then you procrastinate even more and feel even worse. It's a downward cycle.

If you have something important that you have been avoiding, go and do it. It will fill you up with even more energy that will allow you to take even more action.

5. Activities that numb your mind.

There are some activities that we consider as relaxing like watching TV or random videos on the internet. In reality, they numb your mind and slowly drain your emotional energy. How did you feel after watching TV for three hours straight? I feel like something has sucked the life out of me. It becomes so hard to get yourself up to do something afterwards.

Some common mind-numbing activities:

- Watching TV or random online videos.

- Watching the News (nothing but negativity and drama).

- Sitting at your computer for a long time (i.e., video games)

- Wasting your time on social media ("What's Suzy doing? Let's check her status.")

- Having lots of sugar and carbohydrates in meals (the energy crash you get after an hour is massive)

Such activities slowly drain your energy; therefore making it harder for you to stop. Once you feel drained, you just keep on watching TV because it keeps your attention away from your body, which is feeling bad (drained out).

The more you watch, the more your mind numbs, the worse you feel, so you keep watching TV to avoid focusing on how bad you feel. Your mind keeps you engaged with TV because it wants to avoid the painful experience of real life.

Be very careful with all of these activities. Most of them are like quicksand, the more you engage, the deeper you sink, and the harder it becomes to come out.

Try to make changes in your lifestyle based on the information provided. Avoid activities that drain your emotional energy and take out time to rejuvenate emotional energy. You will feel more alive and vibrant. Your productivity will get a huge jump. You will be more social person and, best of all, you will feel happy and alive for most of your day.

Isn't that something we all crave?

51 WAYS TO INCREASE YOUR HAPPINESS

There are several big and small things you can do to increase your happiness. Some make a huge difference while others make smaller impacts. But they all count. Here are 51 different ways to increase your happiness.

1. Practice gratitude

Do the 5-minute gratitude exercise mentioned in chapter 1. The idea behind gratitude is this - be *thankful* for what you have, and you'll end up having more things to be thankful for. If you concentrate on what you don't have, you'll ever have enough.

2. Physical exercise

Doing physical exercise release endorphins and several other *'feel-good'* hormones in the body which make you feel happier and positive.

3. Listen to your favorite music

When you listen to the kind of music you like, the brain releases dopamine, a neurotransmitter which makes you feel happy and energized. Next time you need a boost in your emotional energy, listen to your favorite music for 15 minutes.

4. Smile & laugh

When you are feeling down, try smiling. There's a good chance your mood will change for the better. Even a forced smile can trick the brain into elevating your mood because of the connection between smile and happiness in the brain.

5. Help other people

Helping others makes you feel great because the brain releases feel-good chemicals which psychologists call "helper's high." It motivates you to perform more acts of kindness.

6. Connect with people

Connecting with people every day will make you feel great. Face to face interactions are the best, but calls, text messages, emails also work great.

7. Create an empowering morning ritual

I cannot stress enough the importance of having a morning routine. It will set you up for a productive and joy-filled day.

8. Travel to beautiful places

When you travel, you experience things that you had never experienced before. You see beautiful places and landscapes. You meet memorable people. You try fun activities that you have never tried before.

9. Write a journal

Journaling can improve your mood and give you a greater sense of emotional well-being and happiness.

10. Get a pet

Any pet owner will tell you how much they love their pets and how happy it makes them. The loving touch of a furry or scaly family member at the end of a long, tough day is unlike anything else.

11. Show more compassion

When we feel compassion towards others, it not only makes others feel loved and cared for, but it also helps us to develop inner happiness and peace.

12. Spend more time with happy people

Emotions are contagious! Spending time with happy, upbeat people will rub their positivity on you.

13. Deep belly breathing

Deep belly breathing calms the mind, reduces stress and help in centering yourself. It changes your whole perspective for the better.

14. Read positive quotes

Reading positive quotes daily will make your mind habitual to positive thoughts. It's a great way to elevate your mood and mindset.

15. Read inspirational books

Reading great books will make you grow as a person. It expands your mind and opens up the doors to new ideas and possibilities. It fills you up with hope and enthusiasm about the future.

16. Join a dance class

Along with boosting energy and mood, dancing lowers stress levels similar to aerobic exercises.

17. Start watching comedy

Everybody can use a good laugh and nothing is easier than turning on the TV while sitting on a comfortable couch.

18. Take a short walk outside

Like any other physical exercise, walking outside increases blood flow which releases endorphins to make us feel good. It also exposes us to greenery, fresh air, and sunshine which make us feel even better.

19. Be kind to others

What goes around comes around. It is especially true with kindness. Research shows that being kind to others increases our happiness as well as theirs.

20. Imagine best-case scenarios

Whether we make lemonade out of lemons or complain about lemons, we always have a choice. Optimists see opportunities. Pessimists make excuses. Optimism boosts our overall happiness and enthusiasm.

21. Spend time in nature

In May of 2013, 10,000 Canadians participated in David Suzuki Foundation's 30x30 challenges. After the challenge, participants reported feeling happier, relaxed and more productive after spending time in nature.

22. Watch sunrise

The sunrise is beautiful. The subtle changes in the sky as the sun rises over the mountains, trees, and houses are breathtaking. It fills you up with joy.

23. Reduce your traffic time

Try to live near your workplace. It cuts down your daily traffic time significantly. You can use that spare time doing something you really like.

24. Sufficient quality sleep

Sleep makes or breaks your day. It has a huge impact on your mood and energy levels during the day. A bad night's sleep will make you irritable and groggy. While a quality sleep will make you positive, upbeat and full of energy.

25. Practice mindfulness

Mindfulness can help you get out of the negative thoughts loop while being more compassionate to others, increasing your overall happiness.

26. Talk to your good friends

When you feel down, talk to your friends. A friend is someone who makes you laugh even when you think you'll never smile again.

27. Join a yoga class

Yoga reduces stress, anxiety, anger, and fatigue which inhibit happiness and makes you present to the moment. It is an excellent practice for improving your overall emotional wellbeing.

28. Create a new empowering habit

Empowering habits lay the foundation of a happy and successful life. Bad ones do the opposite.

29. Compliment yourself for small things

Giving compliments to self are a great way to boost your self-confidence and self-esteem. It boosts your overall happiness.

30. Schedule an hour for things you love

Take an hour in your day for your hobbies, or things that you want to do. Taking out time for yourself feels amazing!

31. Do something creative: write, paint, etc.

Doing something creative gives us a break from our daily routines, helping us express emotions and boosts our happiness levels.

32. Overcome a fear you have

Facing and then overcoming something you were previously afraid of is one of the best feelings in the world. You really feel like you have grown as a person. But be careful with it. Some fears like fear of fire and fear of a snake bite are good for you. It keeps you away from harm.

33. Forgive yourself & others for past mistakes

Forgiving yourself reduces the emotional baggage in your heart and makes you free from past events. It is one of the best healing practices you can do to improve your happiness and joy.

34. Take a small step towards your goal

Taking action brings progress. Making progress makes you feel good. You feel good and take even more action. It's an upward cycle of growth and happiness.

35. Thank the universe for everything

Being thankful shields you from negativity, eliminates stress, provides healing and make you happier.

36. Find your strengths

Finding your hidden strengths and talents can be so fulfilling. There are so many methods available in the market today that will help you find your unique gifts. A simple Google search is all that is needed.

37. Be proactive

Missing opportunities due to laziness feels terrible. We regret not doing the right thing when we had the time. In turn, proactively tackling our responsibilities fills us with positive emotions.

38. Be more accepting of yourself

Only with self-acceptance can you make efforts to change yourself. Say "I like myself." Self-acceptance is the first step toward expressing self-love and happiness.

39. Use your natural talents & strengths

We all have unique talents or strengths. Using our gifts allow us to unlock our true potential. While we are utilizing our strengths, we get so immersed in the act that we forget the sense of time and become completely present. There are no worries at the moment. Our mind is laser-focused and happy.

40. Express love to your close ones

Expressing your love to people near and dear to your heart is one of the best feelings in the world. Remember the last time you expressed your love to another person. How were you feeling at the time? Best feeling ever, right?

41. Never compare yourself with others

Comparisons with other people create distance between us and them. It is an unhealthy habit that should be dropped immediately. When you do not compare yourself with others and accept yourself as you are and them as they are, you feel more empathic and connected to the world around you.

42. Encourage others to do their best

Encouraging words make a difference. Right words spoken at the right time have the power to change lives. Try to encourage other people when they need it. It might help them overcome a difficult challenge and make you feel proud of yourself.

43. Live by your principles

Our values drive our behavior and actions. They determine what is important to us and help us move towards our goals. Knowing and living by our values help us to make right decisions and promote joy in our life.

44. Drop all judgments towards other people

Studies have shown that we need strong social relationships to be physically and emotionally healthy. The habit of judging other people is one of the biggest obstacles in forming harmonious social bonds. Drop all judgment towards self and other people.

45. Focus on what you want in your life

Tony Robbins quotes, "focus on what you want, not on what you don't want." When we focus on our desires, we feel hopeful and excited. If we focus on something we dislike, we feel worried and anxious. To live a joy-filled life must take control of our focus and put it on the things we like and want.

46. Donate to charity

There's an old Chinese proverb: "If you want happiness for an hour, take a nap. If you want happiness for a day, go fishing. If you want happiness for a year, inherit a fortune. If you want happiness for a lifetime, help somebody." Happiness is found in helping others.

47. Buy experiences rather than stuff

People say money cannot buy happiness. That is true if you use the money to buy stuff. But if you use the money to buy an experience, the pleasant memories could stay in your mind to be cherished forever. Even after many years have passed, you can relive those happy moments each time you think about it.

48. Always do your best

Integrity is one of the core values which define our happiness. Even in difficult times, do your best. Because even if you didn't get the result you wanted, you could say to yourself, "I gave it my best shot. There is nothing more I could have done." There will be peace in your mind.

49. Drop the mind-reading habit

This is another bad habit which deteriorates our relationships. Never assume what the other person is thinking. Because 99% of the time, we are wrong. Eventually, it leads to conflict. So to build long-lasting, harmonious relationships, get rid of the mind-reading habit.

50. Get a new hobby

Hobbies are a lot of fun. They provide a break from the everyday mundane activities. Try a new hobby. It will bring a much-needed novelty to the day.

51. Live a healthy lifestyle

Health is everything. Good health allows us to experience various joys of life - fun, laughter, wealth, good relationships, hobbies, etc. Living a healthy lifestyle makes up the foundation for everything else, including happiness. Make it a priority.

Final Thoughts

We all want to be happy. But we confuse pleasure with happiness. Both of these – pleasure and happiness – provide good feelings to the individual, but there is a big difference between them.

Pleasure is temporary. It is only a momentary feeling of enjoyment, which is dependent on the present experience. If you are watching a good movie, you feel good. But those good feelings will go away as soon as the movie gets over.

That is not happiness. That's pleasure. True happiness is not a temporary fix.

We have been so brainwashed by the social media and advertisements that we tend to believe happiness is buying that expensive car, or that piece of property, or those branded cloths. All of these are good. All of these have merit if they are coming from the right place.

If we look at money, fame, and lifestyle to fill the void inside and make us feel happy, it will never work. Such is the nature of pleasure. The good feelings are always fleeting in nature. If we want to feel happy in our everyday life, we cannot depend on these worldly things.

Why?

Because they are not permanent themselves. Money comes and goes. Fame comes and goes. We cannot rely upon external things to make us happy. They all can be and will be taken away from us at one point.

They are not a stable source of happiness. We cannot depend on them for our happiness.

True happiness comes from within. It's so counterintuitive. We have been conditioned since childhood that happiness is in getting good grades, dressing well, pleasing others, doing what everybody tells you to do, and being a good boy or girl.

It all worked in childhood. Most of our social conditioning is good. But many times, it holds us back from living a life we deserve. If we want to be happy, we need to take action. We need to make our own decisions. We need to connect with other people. We have to look at the world from a different perspective.

It all seems daunting for the person reading this the first time, but it's not. Actually, we all can learn to be happier in our daily life.

Happiness is a learnable skill

Just like with any skill, such as learning guitar, skating, yoga, cooking... happiness can also be learned. You can learn to be happier.

In this modern life that we live, we have lost touch with happiness. We have become so focused on doing and achieving, that we have forgotten how to feel good.

The solution is to practice being happy on a daily basis. Use the tools and information mentioned in this book to aid you.

We have a network of neural pathways inside our brain. Every behavior is designated to a specific set of neural pathways. As we repeat a behavior over and over, the neural pathways grow and become larger.

The larger a neural pathway becomes, the more signals it allows to pass through. The more neural signals pass through, the easier it becomes for us to indulge in the behavior.

Repetition is the key here. The more we repeat a skill or behavior, the easier it becomes.

We need to do that with being happy. People who have a large neural pathway for happiness tend to access that state of mind frequently during the day. They find it easy to be happy for even smallest of reasons.

The more we practice being happy, the easier it becomes. At some point, we can reach a place where we feel happy for the majority of our day.

Isn't that the holy grail? Most of the people I meet say that if only they can feel a bit more happiness in the day... everything would be perfect.

That is why I wrote this book. I lost touch with happiness. I lost it all for a career. In my blind drive to achieve more, I sacrificed happiness and enjoyment. After some time, it became harder for me to feel happy. It would take an extremely well put together joke to make me laugh.

And whenever I did laugh, it was only for a 2–3 seconds. Then I automatically went back to my straight, expressionless face. I started to feel weird. Whenever I did meet my old friends and family, I felt so out of place. "Everyone is laughing and having fun... Why not me? What's wrong with me?" I asked myself.

I felt something needed to change. That feeling turned into an absolute necessity when doctors told me that over-stress was the reason behind the headache I had been experiencing over the last few months. I began to take things easy and started looking for ways to get in touch with happiness again.

I did go back to my natural, happier self... and this whole book is about how I did it and I wholeheartedly believe that if I can do it, you can too.

You have just learned several powerful concepts and exercises to build an unshakable, rock-solid sense of positivity & happiness. These are some of my most cherished tools & information for building optimism and joy. I have extensively used these to change my thought process from negative to a positive one.

Now it's up to you to take this knowledge and use it wisely. Remember: without its application, knowledge has no value. But when acted upon, it has the power to change your destiny.

Use this information well, and it will continue to serve you forever.

I wish you all the happiness, love, and success that you truly deserve.

All the best.

Vishal Pandey
Yourselfactualization@gmail.com

If you have enjoyed this book, please take a moment to put an honest review on the website from where you have purchased this book. Your review will be very valuable for getting this book to reach more people who need this information.

Thank you.

About The Author

Vishal Pandey was born in Lucknow, India. After completing post graduation in management, he joined corporate world, only to realize quickly that it was not the path for him. His decade old passion for self development led him to the world of writing and creation of his blog.

Over the course of fourteen years, he read hundreds of books, listened to audio/video programs, attended seminars on the topic of personal development and tested every piece of information by applying it in real life.

His blog was originally created to share this information with the world, but later evolved into a platform for mutual interaction with his readers. After receiving several requests to write a book from his readers, he wrote 'Success Code', followed by 'Positive Thinking' and 'Social Success'.

Besides writing, he loves meditation, yoga, martial arts, music, nutrition, psychology & behavior and travelling.

You can contact him at:

Email: yourselfactualization@gmail.com

Facebook: facebook.com/selfactualization.co

Twitter: @selfactualized9

More Books by Vishal Pandey

Positive Thinking: How to Stop Focusing on Nonsense and Live a Better Life

The Power of Positive Energy: How to declutter your mind, control emotions, manage stress, and rewire your brain by letting go of fear and anxiety

Success Code: Gold Standard Principles for Achieving Success

Social Success: Be Likeable, Create Instant Rapport and Influence People

The Magic of Positive Thinking

Gratitude: Getting In Touch With What Really Matters

Forgiveness: The Greatest Cure for a Suffering Heart

The Art of Relationship: Secrets of Long Lasting Fulfilling Relationships

More books by Vishal Pandey:

Positive Thinking: How to stop focusing on nonsense and live a better life

Are you deeply unsatisfied with your current life situation?

Is it hard for you to feel motivated?

Are you having trouble with self-doubt and negative inner thoughts?

Do you really want to fix the situation but cannot make yourself take action?

This book has the answers you seek.

Vishal Pandey, author of Positive Thinking, is not a self-help guru. He is a regular guy who was fighting with depression, negative thoughts, self-doubt, and procrastination for thirteen long years. Determined to break out of it, he tried out every possible advice, method, and technique under the sun and finally managed to do it. This book is about the best advice and practices he found in those thirteen years to break the habit of constant negative thoughts which dragged down his spirit and potential.

Backed up by a combination of science and philosophy, Positive Thinking has helped hundreds of readers break the habit of negative thinking & self-doubt. Filled with inspiring stories, smart advice, and practical exercises outlined in clear & actionable steps, every chapter is designed to help you think and change the way you live.

Discover:

~ How to control your negative thoughts and experience more joy, peace & fulfillment?

~ How to live by your own rules and focus only on things which are meaningful & important?

~ How to stop making excuses and feel motivated to take action every day?

~ How to develop rock solid self-confidence?

~ How to stop sweating over small stuff that ultimately doesn't matter at all?

~ How to get out of your head and crush feelings of self-doubt & inferiority?

~ How to handle negative, toxic people and their comments? They will never have any effect on you.

~ How to stop feeling stuck and be inspired to start moving ahead in life?

~ How to break the habit of procrastination and laziness once and for all?

~ How to never let past rejections & failure bother you again?

Praise for the book:

~ "Brings change at the deepest level" - Review by Reader's Favorite, one of the largest book review organizations in the world.

~ "I strongly recommend this book. He has tackled various issues in an uncomplicated manner. An absolute must read which doesn't drag too much."

~ "As I read this book I could see a lot of the traits of a negative personality in myself. The way to make changes is easily defined in this book. The author gives very simple and clear guidelines on how to make changes in your mindset to ultimately make positive changes in your life. Don't just read it and forget it. Start a journal and begin to see life in a positive light!"

~ "I couldn't believe he had never written a book before....this one is better than 90% of all that I have read. Would highly recommend it."

Do not give up on your dreams. The life you want is only a decision away. Either you could continue to be the way you are now OR you could do something to change it.

More books by Vishal Pandey:

The Power of Positive Energy: How to declutter your mind, control emotions, manage stress, and rewire your brain by letting go of worry and anxiety

Do you want to be more positive and confident in your everyday life?

Do you imagine yourself FREE from negative self-talk and filled with joy, fulfillment, peace, and passion every day?

The sole purpose of The Power of Positive Energy is to help you break the habit of negative thinking & self-doubt. Filled with inspiring stories, smart advice, and practical exercises outlined in clear & actionable steps, you will get to know the exact steps on how to make yourself happy, inspired, thankful, peaceful, content, and optimistic.

You will discover various tools and ideas to completely transform your mindset and life:

- 7 Powerful ways to supercharge your life with positivity

- The perfect morning routine to make you happy and productive all-day

- 6 Simple ways to boost motivation at work and life

- How to raise your positive vibrations and attract what you need

- How to start a gratitude practice and change your life

- 4 Secrets to live a happier, more fulfilling life every day

- 8 Hacks you can do to boost self-confidence

- How to truly forgive someone who has hurt you

- How to live a healthier (and happier) lifestyle

- Simple habits to make yourself happy and peaceful every day

Here are the ultimate benefits you will get out of this book:

- You will become more optimistic

- You will be more positive and confident in your everyday life

- You will have a morning routine that supercharges your productivity and happiness

- You will stay motivated and focused all the time

- You will be able to let go of all anger by forgiving people who hurt you in the past

- You will have a clear understanding of who you are and what makes you happy

- You will be more grateful and blissful every day

- You will live a healthier lifestyle

- You will be a calm and peaceful person

If you want to experience more love, joy, peace, and fulfillment in your daily life, get the book now.

More Books by Vishal Pandey:

Success Code: Gold standard principles for achieving success

Do you want to cut the noise and find out what <u>really produces results in real life</u>? Are you <u>overwhelmed</u> by the amount of information available? Are you looking for a <u>proven, reality based system</u> which will show you how to start strong, make consistent progress, achieve your goals and everything in between?

Get up-close-and-personal view of what really creates success

It took YEARS to build the PERFECT SYSTEM...

On his quest to find the key elements behind success in modern world, author spent 14 years studying and examining diverse success strategies, with only one question in mind -

"Will it produce results in real world scenario?"

Success Code is a collection of these marked pieces of information. This book will introduce you to a practical, reality-based program designed to <u>break through all barriers</u> and <u>lead you to the results</u> you really want.

What you will learn inside Success Code?

- Discover the ACTUAL PRINCIPLES which create the success you want. No fluff. Only hard-hitting, result producing principles and practices.

- Unlock the step-by-step blueprint for beginning, making progress, destroying obstacles, achieving desired objective and everything in between.

- DESTROY your limiting beliefs, for good.

- Build rock-solid belief in your success even BEFORE you achieve it.

- Start strong, and quickly ADVANCE to the NEXT LEVEL.

- How to maintain your mood and energy to ensure CONSTANT PROGRESS?

- How to LET GO of the PAST and focus on a better FUTURE?

- CRUSH your doubts and fears.

- Learn powerful, proven concepts to INCREASE your MOTIVATION.

- The RIGHT way to take action and MAXIMIZE your results.

- BRAINWASH your mind into positivity and growth, regardless of your current situation.

- See what YOUR SUCCESS looks like, so you know what to AIM for.

- Stop beating a dead horse and EMBRACE the change.

- How to use POWER of MOMENTUM in your favor?

- Master the art of focus and disciple.

Get the full Repertoire of tools and skills you NEED in order to achieve the results you want.

What to expect from Success Code, if you are a beginner:

- You will tell yourself "Wow! I CAN do this. It looks POSSIBLE!"

What to expect from Success Code, if you are a veteran:

- A revisit to the BEST principles and practices available, from a fresh perspective.

 Becoming successful is the gateway to happiness and joy filled life. Not only you get what you desire but it also allows you to help other people and contribute to the society. Your self esteem and sense of confidence will soar knowing you have tapped into your full potential and achieved what you set out to achieve. You pass on this knowledge to other people - helping them succeed - thus making your contribution in creating a better world to live in.

You have the potential to achieve all that you desire, right now. Success Code will show you the HOW.

Printed by Amazon Italia Logistica S.r.l.
Torrazza Piemonte (TO), Italy